Middle Management in Action

Practical Approaches to School Improvement

ERIC RUDING

London and New York

First published 2000
by RoutledgeFalmer
11 New Fetter Lane, London EC4P 4EE

Simultaneously published in the USA and Canada
by RoutledgeFalmer
29 West 35th Street, New York, NY 10001

RoutledgeFalmer is an imprint of the Taylor & Francis Group

© 2000 Eric Ruding

The right of Eric Ruding to be identified as the Author of this Work has
been asserted by him in accordance with the Copyright,
Designs and Patents Act 1988

Typeset in Sabon by
Keystroke, Jacaranda Lodge, Wolverhampton
Printed and bound in Great Britain by
TJ International Ltd, Padstow, Cornwall

British Library Cataloguing in Publication Data
A catalogue record for this book is available from the British Library

Library of Congress Cataloguing in Publication Data
A catalogue record for this book has been requested

ISBN 0–415–23155–8

To Carol, Andrew, Alison Sarah,
Alison Claire and Connie

Contents

Figures

Tables

Acknowledgements

My thanks must go to Dr Marie Brown, the Director of the Centre for Continuing Professional Development in the School of Education at the University of Manchester, for her help, support and encouragement, particularly at the early stages of preparation. I would also wish to thank Margaret Lloyd, Head of Green Lane School, and David Wilson, Deputy Head at Sale Grammar School (both Trafford LEA), for reading the earlier drafts of the book and for their reviews of the completed manuscript. Their comments and suggestions for improvement have been incorporated and have added greatly to the value of the book as a practical aid in schools.

Many of the ideas and materials presented here have developed over the years I have been involved in the in-service training of teachers at all levels and my thanks must also go to colleagues and to the many teachers, particularly in Trafford LEA, who have helped in the formulation and trial of these ideas.

Introduction

Until recently the term 'middle management' has rarely been used in schools although 'posts of extra responsibility' have existed for many years. Traditionally these posts were, in the main, for subject responsibility in secondary schools (e.g. heads of subject or department) or for parts of the school (e.g. head of nursery or infants in primary schools or heads of year in secondary schools). Similarly, other posts were for specific aspects of the work of the school (e.g. careers in secondary or games in primary schools). The posts of responsibility were for additional duties beyond the teaching commitment and did not usually involve contributing to the management of the whole school. This was in contrast to middle management posts in other organisations, where the incumbents are expected to contribute to the management of the whole organisation. Interview evidence from schools which formed part of Manchester University research (Brown *et al.* 1999) indicated that, in schools which have discussed and developed management structures, middle managers are perceived as:

- the channel of communication between senior staff and classroom teachers;
- those responsible for the preparation of pastoral-based responses to policies and strategies initiated by the senior management team;
- guiding a system of working upwards from departmental staff and reflecting upwards their contributions to whole school development planning.

Different government agencies have suggested that this kind of leadership is suitable for middle managers in schools in the future. The responsibilities put forward by the Welsh Office (1994) included fostering the knowledge, skills, understanding and attitudes of teachers; developing the vision of the department through the encouragement of team work and the use of meetings to plan, share and discuss policy and methods. The Teacher Training Agency (TTA 1996) offered a similar list but linked it more firmly to management roles through a framework which involves vision and target setting, monitoring, evaluation and an improvement programme.

However, changes introduced by more recent legislation, notably the National Curriculum and its assessment, have led to a significant change in the nature of such posts and, in many schools, the functions of those with such responsibilities. In all schools, the range of these posts has increased and the expectations of the post-holders have changed. In secondary schools, in addition to the role of the head of year or department/subject, there are other middle management posts (e.g. heads of key stage or lower school) and, in primary and special schools, there are curriculum co-ordinators and key stage co-ordinators. The National Curriculum and its development in schools has also led to the establishment of other across-school responsibilities (e.g. special educational needs co-ordinators – SENCOs; co-ordinators for assessment, recording and reporting; and co-ordinators for information and communications technology).

The publication *National Standards for Subject Leaders* (TTA 1998), which is referred to throughout this book, gives too narrow a view of the middle management roles as they now exist in schools. In addition, the majority of what is written about the subject leader's role is equally applicable to the other middle management roles. Thus, throughout this book, the generic terms 'team' and 'team leader' are used, rather than head of department/subject, except where there is need to make reference to a specific function. The term 'team leader' includes all those with responsibility for leading a team of teachers working on any aspect of the work of a school. Heads of department are perceived as having a bridging or brokering role in which they translate the school's objectives into the plans and programmes to be delivered through the subject areas of the curriculum.

Both recent research on the role of middle managers (Brown *et al.* 1999) and evidence from OFSTED (1997) on subject management in secondary schools have highlighted the following areas as being key to the development of effective leadership and management at this level (see also *Supplements KE3* and *KE4*):

- Headteachers, other senior managers and governors may work hard to develop good leadership, vision and a strong sense of purpose within a school but a committed and effective middle management which shares in whole school decision-making is also essential;
- Where lines of communication with senior management are not clear, where the roles of middle managers are not sufficiently defined, and where senior managers do not monitor the implementation of whole school policies at team/department/subject level, such teams tend to act autonomously, to set vague or unrealistic targets, and so progress towards raising achievement is patchy and unco-ordinated;
- The exercise of the role of the middle manager is increasingly effective but remains uneven in most schools;
- Improvement in middle management has been less marked than that of senior management and good practice at this level is not yet sufficiently widespread;
- Some of the more formal strategies (e.g. monitoring and evaluation of teaching and learning) are only gradually being introduced;
- Clear and concise departmental documentation, which is essential, should be used as working material and should be reviewed regularly;
- Planning by members of the team should be based on shared values – effective teaching and learning depends upon the ability of middle managers to motivate, inspire and support teams of staff;
- There is a danger of sub-cultures existing, which are often separate and sometimes different from the culture of the school fostered by the school management team;
- Senior managers can do more to encourage effective middle management by setting a clear framework of expectation and by offering more support (e.g. in the monitoring and evaluation of the work of the department or team);
- Accountability is developed most effectively in schools where there is a clearly specified line management structure, with the head of department or faculty

reporting directly to a member of the school management team, so enabling issues for departmental discussion to be identified and for progress in meeting departmental development objectives to be monitored, assessed and evaluated;

• Middle managers can offer more than is presently found in the development of whole school policies and practices;

• Many heads of department/subject are assiduous in monitoring some aspects of their team's work, such as exercise books, planning schedules and records, but more needs to be done on the more direct monitoring of the learning and teaching;

• For the development of effective middle managers there is a need for further training;

• If middle managers are to carry out more effectively the expansive role identified in the *National Standards* document, they will require sufficient non-teaching time.

The core purpose of the middle manager's role may been defined as:

> To provide professional leadership and management for a subject, or aspect of work of the school, in order to secure high quality teaching, effective use of resources and improved standards of learning and achievement for all pupils.
>
> (Adapted from *National Standards for Subject Leaders*, TTA 1998)

Although the TTA document refers to subject leaders, the vast majority of the issues covered in this book apply to any middle manager who has responsibility for a specific aspect or area of the work of a school. The processes identified throughout are equally applicable to the work of Year Tutors, Heads of House, Key Stage Co-ordinators and indeed anyone who has responsibility for working in, or with, a team. Many of the processes described, of necessity, mirror those that are used for the development of whole school policies and documentation and one of the aims of the book is to help middle managers to become more involved in the development of whole school initiatives. Recent research (Brown *et al.* 1999) has shown that middle managers in many schools have little involvement in the planning of whole school issues, which not only is a waste of expertise but also misses the opportunity for further professional development of middle managers, particularly those aspiring to more senior responsibilities. However, some senior management teams feel that middle managers spend too much time in administration and that they treat this as a refuge rather than face becoming involved in a newer role within evaluation and staff development. This suggests that training, which so far has often been concentrated on skills development, should be redirected to enable middle managers to understand these new roles.

In addition, many of the aspects of this book will provide guidance for all teachers in their own planning, as there is a concentration on the processes involved rather than on the level of that planning. Detail is given in some sections which would seem to apply more to whole school requirements than to team or departmental ones. This detail is included where there are some direct and indirect effects on the work of teams and, in some cases, individual teachers. Additionally, those middle managers aspiring to senior management posts should find the detail valuable in identifying some of the issues which must be faced in the strategic development of whole school issues. A key element throughout is the need for the department/team to follow closely whole school policies and documentation in the areas described. Whilst each department/team will develop its own culture and way of working this must never vary so much that it falls outside, or conflicts with, that which the headteacher and governors have determined for the whole school. Where this sort of possible conflict occurs it is often because the team/department leader has been insufficiently involved in the process of whole school policy formulation or review.

If there are to be any changes in middle management career development opportunities these, perhaps, should be tied into an analysis of the knowledge and competence required, and an audit of individual capability, together with the opportunity to exercise professionalism in team leadership. The Teacher Training Agency framework offers possible patterns for future organisation of the work of middle managers but awareness of the framework and its contents is still limited among middle managers. 'Training by doing' is still little more than a rite of passage for many aspiring school staff. Unless there is adaptation to a new professionalism, middle managers may continue to be little more than administrators who apply policies within schools.

In the short term, these issues have implications for the establishment of more coherent and targeted development programmes for staff within schools. They also have implications for the TTA and its subject leadership framework, which does not reflect the management needs of those in middle management positions who have whole school and less specific administrative responsibilities. As the demands on middle managers increase, so, inevitably, do their development needs. Research at Manchester University (Brown *et al.* 1999) showed that, in addition to the 'traditional' needs which relate largely to ' managing the department' on a day-to-day basis, there are now needs relating to whole school policy and development.

Part 1 of the book covers all aspects of the roles, responsibilities and statutory duties of middle managers (e.g. the National Curriculum and its assessment). Part 2, in a number of supplements, contains additional information, greater detail and further guidance on some of the more important aspects of the role. Most of the supplements are in the form of exercises which should be useful in the initial audit phase of development planning when new policies and procedures are being formulated or existing ones being reviewed. In addition, the supplements should be useful in helping existing middle managers to identify their own further training needs and those of the team, and in helping aspiring middle managers to identify priorities for their professional development.

The Supplements are grouped and numbered under headings relating to the various aspects of the middle manager's role that are described in Part 1:

KE = Key Elements of the Role of Middle Managers
P   = Planning Processes
CA = Curriculum and Assessment
TL   = Teaching and Learning
S   = Staffing Issues
M   = Other Management Issues

Marie Brown and Bill Boyle
School of Education, University of Manchester

Part 1

School Improvement Strategies

MANAGEMENT OF CHANGE *(Supplement P3)*

There are several methods by which organisations, largely commercial and industrial, have sought to improve practice through a planned process of change. These methods have increasingly been used by schools in order to deal with the growing quest for quality in education such as is outlined in the Parents' Charter. The series of Education Acts, culminating in the Education Reform Act 1988, has meant that schools have moved nearer to the clients they serve. Central government, in its own words, has sought 'to improve the quality of teaching and learning in schools by the introduction of market forces, choice and competition into the education system'. This has led to schools being more accountable as a result of:

- the diminished role and function of LEAs in line with the increasing transfer of decisions to schools;
- the introduction of Local Management of Schools (LMS) by the end of 1993 through which schools' delegated budgets are largely determined by pupil numbers;
- the publication of league tables for external examination and test results;
- OFSTED inspections and the subsequent publication of the findings, including the naming of 'failing schools';
- benchmarking and target setting for schools and their pupils;
- a revised scheme for teacher appraisal which is likely to be further strengthened by the introduction of new regulations on pay and performance review;
- the publication of national qualifications or standards for teachers;
- the National Curriculum and its assessment arrangements;
- open enrolment, leading to a need for managing parental choice procedures;
- increased competition for pupils and the money they generate.

Schools are therefore much in the market place, where parents* who are pleased with the 'product' will continue to choose and support certain schools and so these schools will generate income. On the other hand, schools appearing to produce an 'inferior product' will lose or fail to gain pupils and the money that comes with them.

---

* Throughout this book any reference to 'parent' or 'parents' includes others with parental responsibilities.

Most teachers welcome change when it adds variety to some of the daily and annual routines that they face and when they are involved in the decisions on, or processes of, such change. However, in recent years the imposition of many radical, external changes has made teachers' lives difficult and, to some, has been quite threatening. This situation has been worsened by continued external criticism and a lack of appreciation of the problems involved, in spite of the enormous progress made. Now, sadly, any positive attempt at improvement through further change is likely to elicit immediate resistance to that change.

What has proved much more successful has been the management of planned change, where schools/teams:

- recognise and understand the need for change;
- assess the timing of, and their readiness for, the change;
- prepare for the planning process;
- are able to resource the planning and the innovation;
- anticipate problems in any transition phase;
- review the planning process;
- monitor implementation of the change;
- evaluate the innovation.

Where schools/teams have long-term ideas for significant change, the change needs to be broken down into smaller, but interdependent changes. Success is more likely with smaller, shorter-term changes and such success often provides the impetus for continuing with the changes. In most planning for change there tends to be periods of uncertainty and frustration where teachers/teams need support and encouragement. Change can be damaging to confidence, so reassurance must be given if the impetus for change is to be maintained.

In planning for change, care must be taken to consider involving appropriate support staff in the school, particularly where the change will have an impact on their work for the school/team. There are instances where it will be valuable to include them in the discussions and planning as their views may add important perspectives to the change. The pupils and their parents also have a part to play in the process and their perceptions can be sought by questionnaires such as those given in *Supplement TL6*.

In considering the planning for change, the following points should prove valuable:

- Change is likely to be successful when people agree with it and/or see that there is a need for it;
- As people tend to mistrust or misunderstand anything which is threatening, there is a need for support, help, reassurance and recognition of success;
- Success is more likely if those affected by the change are involved in the decision to change, in planning the change and subsequently in implementing it;
- Whilst a consensus approach is ideal, change often generates conflict which will need to be managed as a part of the process;
- Hindrances to change must be recognised and taken into account during the change-planning process;
- Change is, of necessity, a slow process and continued enthusiasm and commitment must be encouraged;
- As there is to be continued external demand for change (e.g. the National

Curriculum in Key Stages 1 and 2 in the year 2000 and a revised system for pay and performance review), the culture of the school and the teams within it need to accept and maintain change as a way of life.

QUALITY ASSURANCE INITIATIVES

Initiatives such as Total Quality Management (TQM) and BS 5750, which are used by industrial or commercial organisations, have begun to find their way into the educational sphere. These consist of a philosophy by which the organisation can produce quality goods and/or services through either quality control or quality assurance. Quality control means inspecting outputs and rejecting anything which falls below a certain standard; school inspections and school self-evaluation techniques are examples of this approach. Quality assurance, on the other hand, involves designing systems to deliver quality before the event; initial and in-service training of teachers is one aspect of quality assurance.

One of the essential bases of TQM is the concept of Kaizen. This is derived from two Japanese words, *kai* meaning 'change', and *zen* meaning 'good' (for the better), i.e. improvement though change. One of the leading exponents of Kaizen, the Chairman of the airline SAS, once said that he wanted the airline to be better by 1 per cent in a 100 ways, rather than 100 per cent better in one way, and that the 1 per cent improvement had to be continuous. This amount is suitable for any complex organisation, such as a school, where there are many interacting factors, all of which contribute to the organisation's success (or lack of it).

A quality assurance process for teaching would work backwards from any teacher with any class to find out the prerequisites to ensure that:

- the teacher is suitably qualified, experienced and knowledgeable;
- it is an appropriate group of pupils;
- appropriate material is being taught;
- sufficient and relevant teaching and learning resources are available;
- the time is appropriate;
- the teaching space is appropriate.

Each of these would be checked to identify what was necessary for there to be a high expectation that it would be fulfilled. The key element is 'right first time' and as little as possible would be left to chance.

(Adapted from Fidler 1996)

Using this approach, quality assurance should be the essential feature of all development planning in schools. In summary, quality assurance is about:

- fitness for purpose;
- shared understanding and purposes between all partners;
- regularly questioning and challenging assumptions;
- turning rhetoric into policies for action;
- planning and making decisions based on accurate information;
- empowering teams and individuals.

The features of quality are:

- Quality is easy to aspire to but difficult to define;
- A concern for quality is everyone's responsibility and attention to detail matters;
- Consensus about quality may be difficult to achieve;
- Shared values, philosophy, culture and purposes are vital to a sense of quality;
- Quality is not achieved merely by describing it on paper;
- Narrowing the gap between rhetoric and reality is a major concern;
- Other audiences will determine many aspects of perceived quality.

The features of quality in school and middle management are:

- The quality of pupils' learning is at the heart of effective management;
- All management should be focused on this;
- All teachers are managers;
- School management practices should be free of bias and discrimination;
- Effective school management should emphasise:
  - shared mission, vision and values;
  - consultation, participation and teamwork;
  - accountability;
  - a concern for quality.

Aspects of quality assurance in relation to working with teams are given in *Supplement S3*.

Other quality assurance processes which will be familiar to schools are:

- Staff development (see *Supplements P1* and *S2*);
- OFSTED inspections of schools (see p. 21);
- School Based Review mechanisms, including GRIDS which is widely used in primary schools and is a process model using instruments to undertake investigation;
- Management Competencies, which attempt to identify the skills necessary in jobs and whether these are apparent in practice; the tasks/skills/attributes approach is used in the training under the Headteacher Leadership and Management Programme (HEADLAMP), the National Professional Qualification for Headship (NPQH) and the Leadership Programme for Serving Headteachers (LPSH) and is also in all of the *National Standards* documents (TTA 1998);
- Investors in People, which provides:
  - a framework for ensuring that all members of a school are familiar with its aims and know the part that they play in the process;
  - a means of development for individuals in order to help them in this;
  - accreditation for the school, which may also contribute to development by providing a form of 'kite mark' of quality.

THE PROCESS OF DEVELOPMENT PLANNING, REVIEW AND EVALUATION (*Supplements P1–P9*)

Before any effective planning can take place there are three vital prerequisites:

   agreed mission, vision and values;
   leadership;
   teamwork.

Mission, Vision and Values

It is important that, under any of these headings, there is a shared and agreed approach to the philosophy of the work of the department/year group/team which, of necessity, must reflect the mission, vision and values of the school. Similarly, where the overall intentions of the school are expressed as aims and objectives, the team's aims and objectives must always concur with these. Examples of statements of a mission and a description of the vision are given on pp. 17–18.

The planning of all developments must be underpinned by the mission and vision and should reflect the culture of the school and the team. This process involves attempting to answer all of the following questions:

- How would you like it (school, department/team or issue) to be?
- What do you really want to achieve?
- Can you picture a better situation?
- In what ways would the situation be better?
- What are the future possibilities?
- Is there agreement about what is needed?

Leadership *(Supplements KE1–KE3)*

In identifying the core purpose of the role of subject leaders, the Teacher Training Agency (1998) sets out a leadership function for those responsible for teams which applies equally well to the role of all middle managers in schools and to all teachers in the context of their particular roles. Evidence from OFSTED (1993–97) shows that the single most important factor in school effectiveness is the quality of leadership at both senior and middle management levels.

The role of the middle manager can be described under the following four headings:

- teacher;
- leader;
- manager;
- administrator.

It could be argued that this is true for all teachers but the most significant role for all school managers is that of leadership. The relationship between the roles of leader, manager and administrator, adapted from Warren Bennis' work (1969), is given in *Supplement KE2* and is further described in the National Standards in *Supplement KE3*.

It is often the practice for the head of department/year/key stage or the subject co-ordinator to be the only person with the leadership role, and in some instances this is a weakness in the system in schools. There is always so much work for the team as a whole to do that it cannot be handled by one person, bearing in mind the teaching commitment that middle managers have to undertake. In the best organisations all staff are expected to adopt a leadership role for parts of the work of the team. This not only spreads the work load but also provides opportunities for professional development and involvement of others in the team. Difficulties arise when a single teacher has subject responsibility and it is important to involve other staff whenever possible (e.g. a member of the school management team, staff from a related subject or others, where the organisation of the school has even a loose faculty structure or grouping of subjects).

Teamwork *(Supplements KE3 and S3)*

Modern management theory propounds the view that teams must form the basis of the process of the management of change or innovation. This allows for the empowerment of members of the team to share in, and therefore take ownership of, the process of development. Again, where one teacher has sole responsibility for a subject or area of work of the school, it is important that there is some way of sharing the task and ideas for development, or at least of using some form of second opinion as the work progresses, possibly through a 'faculty' arrangement, by using a member of the school management team, the LEA Adviser or a colleague in another school.

The Planning Process *(Supplements P1–P7)*

This involves inculcating the view that the process of planning is more important than the plan itself (a good plan may well change but a good planning process should not). The preparation phase provides an excellent opportunity for the involvement of the staff who will have to implement and follow the policies and procedures which are established. It requires a strategy for sharing, and therefore some ownership of, the writing or re-writing of the documentation. This should ensure that everyone has a role to play and a clear remit, including time-constrained targets to be met, through the process of empowerment *(Supplement S1)*. The planning process is cyclical in nature and at its simplest has the stages shown in Figure 1.

However, Figure 1 merely summarises a complex process and, in this form, the four stages tend to have a deal of overlap. Figure 2 shows a more comprehensive picture of the process and the possible interrelationships between each of the stages, which are described in more detail on pp. 12–17. The best example of these interrelationships is the review process which should occur throughout the planning process. Reviewing at stages enables inadequacies to be identified during the process and avoids the frustration of their being identified only at the final evaluation.

Audit/Analysis of Need *(Supplements P9 and CA1)*

This is part of the preparation stage and requires the readiness and commitment of the staff (teaching and support staff). It should involve collection and evaluation of existing plans, policies and documentation.

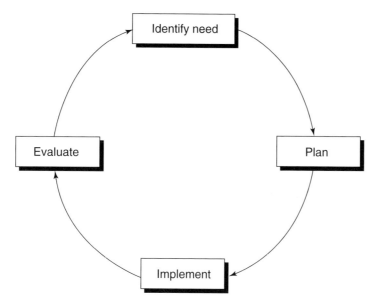

Figure 1 The planning process

Obvious first questions to ask are:

Do any of these need reviewing?
Are there any gaps or out of date items?
Is there any unnecessary duplication?

Where there is no existing policy or procedures documentation, a completely fresh start should be made by discussing and agreeing what needs to be included. The approach suggested in *Supplement CA1* is a useful starting point, although, in order to involve the whole team, a 'brainstorming' approach might be used initially. This is more time consuming but has the benefit of allowing all members of the team to contribute and it creates a sense of ownership from the start of the process. It is unlikely that all policies can be adequately reviewed in any one year but those which are affected by regular change (e.g. the statutory reporting requirements of the National Curriculum and assessment) must be reviewed at least annually. Similarly, whenever a school policy is changed, there is a need to check any changes against the existing departmental/subject policy. Where policies are written as working documents, it should be possible to maintain a continuing review of policies and to make changes during the year. In addition, a list of all existing policies, with dates of the previous reviews, ensures that no policy or procedure is likely to be omitted from the review process.

Analysing Planning Issues *(Supplement P2)*

One technique that has proved valuable in the initial phase of planning is the use of diagramming or mind-mapping to analyse the elements involved in the planning issue being considered. Almost all issues in school or team management are complex and are characterised by a large number of interacting factors operating both inside and outside the school. The 'mapping' approach provides a focus for the planning and is

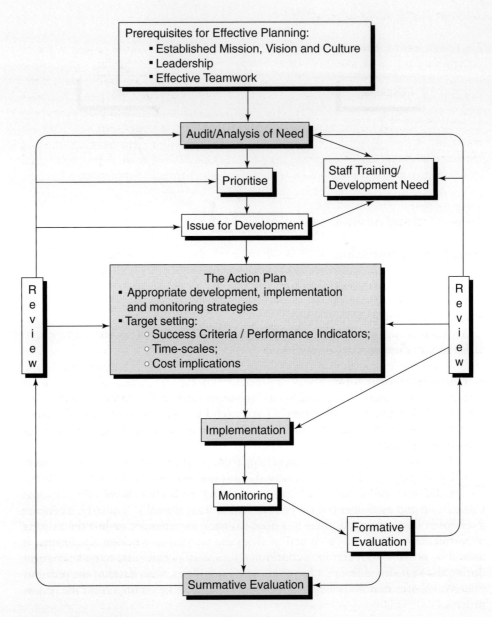

Figure 2 The development planning process

often more time efficient than straight oral or written communication because it is more effective at describing these complex issues.

Action Plans *(Supplement P1)*

Before beginning work on writing or rewriting any part of policy, procedure or documentation, a written and agreed action plan on the particular aspect being considered should be drawn up. This will enable the person with overall responsibility to monitor the process and will allow all of the team to assess the progress made. Action plans are often seen as short-term approaches within the development planning process, dealing with specific issues or with only a part of a longer-term development initiative. Action planning does, however, follow the same steps as the process of longer-term development planning, albeit in an abbreviated form. A proforma used by one primary school for all of its action planning is given in *Supplement P1*.

Target Setting/Ambition *(Supplement CA3)*

If there is to be major change as a result of developments or new policies at subject, school, LEA or national level, it is necessary to decide on the scale and pace of the change. Target setting should include estimates of the timescale and of the time and cost implications. These should be included at the planning stage in order that the ambition of the plan can be evaluated later.

As with target setting for pupils, targets must be demanding but realistic and attainable. Both over-ambition and under-ambition at this stage will lead to frustration and the inevitable lack of effective progress. The production and use of initial trial or draft material will avoid the need for further revisions at the final implementation stage, such as those that occurred with the introduction of the National Curriculum and OFSTED inspections. This approach is usually referred to as formative evaluation, i.e. evaluation at a preliminary stage to inform further planning, and is the process used in establishing pilot schemes.

Performance Indicators and Success Criteria *(Supplement P5)*

At an early stage in the planning process it is necessary to decide on how the success of the initiative is to be measured or assessed on implementation. Performance indicators are not measures in themselves, they simply identify aspects of the work, the levels of which can be judged or measured at intervals (monitoring or formative evaluation) and at the end (summative evaluation). Obvious examples of measurable indicators are reading ages and test and examination results. For indicators which are not easily quantifiable (e.g. attitudes and behaviour of pupils, records of achievement), professional judgements have to be made. A comprehensive list of performance indicators is given in *Supplement P5* but it is important that only a limited number of indicators is used, otherwise the process becomes too complex and it is difficult to separate the effects in analysing the outcomes.

Once indicators are established, the level of expectation for the initiative can be set, i.e. the success criteria can be established. On any development issue the desired outcome should be specific and should be able to be measured or assessed. While many initiatives produce a 'feel good factor', which may be of some value, more accurate measurements or judgements should be included. In setting success criteria, the same principles as those applying to any target setting should be used, i.e. they should be demanding but realistic and attainable within the resources available and the timescales set.

Staff Development *(Supplement S2)*

In the development of initiatives it is important to consider any 'training' which may be needed by members, or indeed all, of the team in order to enable the tasks in the planning process to be completed more effectively. Too often, staff development has been viewed narrowly as individuals attending courses, workshops or conferences. Whilst there are occasions where this is the most appropriate form of training, there are many other approaches, such as visits to other schools who have successfully worked on the same problem, use of LEA staff or other consultants, use of teachers' professional and subject associations. These approaches often allow a much more specific identification of professional development need. An example of a mechanism for the identification of training needs is given in *Supplement P4*.

Review

Once a first draft document is produced, there needs to be a strategy for review, to share views and experiences of the completed work and the process that was used. This will enable the identification of successful approaches or difficulties encountered which might aid future planning.

Reviews should also occur after evaluation or when there is a need to update an existing plan or policy.

Implementation *(Supplement P6)*

Following the first review in the planning process, the new initiative is implemented. In some instances, however, valuable work on planning, which has produced carefully thought out policies on changes, has been followed by a poor implementation phase. It is as though there were a barrier between policy and practice, as if some people felt that the policy were an end point in itself. This has been evident in reports by OFSTED on some whole school policies as well as departmental/subject policies.

Evaluation *(Supplement P7)*

This stage must be related back to the performance indicators and the success criteria identified earlier in the process. Evaluation may be done at intervals (usually referred to as monitoring or formative evaluation) but must be done at the end of the development issue (summative evaluation). It is at this stage that the success, or otherwise, of the initiative can be measured or assessed. Other issues to be considered at the evaluation stage include:

- the cost of the initiative, compared with anticipated cost;
- the time taken compared with the time set for the development;
- the improvement (or lack of it) gained;
- the effect of the development on the pupils, the staff, the school;
- the need for further work on the development issue or related issues.

The principal questions to be answered are: have things improved and has the initiative been economic, efficient and (cost) effective, i.e. 'value for money'?

THE TEAM'S MISSION

This should be a brief statement of the rationale for the teaching of the subject, or within the year group, and must be linked to, and concur with, any mission that the school may have.

The example given below is a generic one which may be expanded briefly to include a subject/year group/key stage context:

> To secure continuous improvement in the quality of the teaching which produces the highest possible standards of pupil achievement and ensures that all pupils develop their knowledge, understanding, skills and abilities within a secure and challenging educational environment.

THE AIMS/VISION OF THE TEAM *(Supplement P8)*

There are two common approaches to setting out the purposes and aspirations of the team, as given in the mission statement: either through a series of aims or through statements of the vision of what the members would like the team to be.

The aims should be broad statements of purpose which reflect the philosophy of the team. Aims are long-term views of what the team aspires to do and to provide for the pupils. Aims are not measurable in that they are broad statements of intent. They are subsequently broken down into shorter-term objectives (intended outcomes) which should be measurable or able to be assessed, i.e. the measures may rely on professional judgement.

The vision is important in that it provides for strategic planning. It is creative and leads to proactive rather than reactive planning. Again the example given below might be modified to include specific issues of particular importance to the subject, year group, key stage or team.

The department/year group/team will have a positive ethos and approach where:

- there is a commitment to high achievement, effective teaching and learning and good relationships;
- the governors, the school management team, staff, pupils and parents have confidence in the leadership and management of the team;
- the teachers recognise accountability for their work and the contribution of the team/department/year group to the development and successful implementation of policies and practices;

- the curriculum effectively promotes pupils' development in as wide a way as possible;
- its effectiveness is kept rigorously under review;
- links with the wider community contribute to pupils' attainment and personal and social development;
- the governors can rely on the team to account for the quality of education that it provides and for the standards that the pupils achieve and to ensure that statutory responsibilities are fulfilled.

The teachers in the team will:

- have a secure knowledge and understanding of the subject(s)/areas being covered;
- set high expectations for pupils;
- plan lessons which address the needs of all pupils within the teaching groups;
- employ the most effective approach for any given content and group of pupils;
- pace lessons appropriately, using time and resources effectively;
- regularly mark and assess pupils' work;
- reinforce and extend pupils' learning and achievement through the setting of consistent and challenging homework;
- manage pupils well and achieve high standards of discipline;
- have their work systematically supported, monitored and evaluated.

The pupils will, at all times, be taught and encouraged to:

- make progress, in relation to prior attainment, to expected (or better than expected) levels;
- show improvement in their literacy, numeracy and information and communications technology skills;
- know the purpose and sequence of activities;
- be well prepared for tests and examinations;
- be enthusiastic about the subject and highly motivated to learn more;
- contribute to the maintenance of a purposeful working environment through their attitudes and behaviour.

The parents will:

- enjoy an effective partnership with the team, which contributes to their children's learning;
- understand and be encouraged to support the work of the team;
- be kept fully informed about their child's achievements and know how they can support and assist their child's progress.

Staff, accommodation, resources and finance will be:

- used economically, efficiently and effectively;
- administered and controlled to ensure best value for money;
- part of carefully costed development plans which are focused on improving educational outcomes

(Adapted from *National Standards for Headteachers*, TTA 1998)

In drawing up the aims or the vision, consideration must be given to the following:

- The aims or vision must accord with the overall aims or vision of the school;
- All members should have the opportunity to contribute; it is crucial that all staff have agreed the statement of aims and/or the vision and have ownership of them; it is also valuable to involve an appropriate member of the school management team in the discussions at some stage, as the team's aims should be agreed by the head and governors;
- The philosophy within the agreed aims/vision should permeate all future discussions which are concerned with putting the policies into practice; this is often the stage where many departments fail;
- Aims or vision should be valid for all pupils; it is when aims/vision are translated into more specific objectives that differentiation for pupils may be necessary and appropriate.

TEAM CULTURE

Culture is defined as

> the characteristic way in which members of an organisation (e.g. school or team) go about their business.

All organisations have a culture. This may be 'strong', i.e. the same assumptions are widely shared, are made obvious and are readily observable, or 'weak', i.e. there are no common, shared beliefs and there is likely to be a lack of agreement on priorities. In effective schools, a positive whole school culture will exist alongside the sub-cultures at departmental/team level. It is important that these sub-cultures do not undermine the overall shared culture of the school. It is possible, even in less effective schools, for individual departments to have a strong culture. In effective schools, the strong culture gives a feeling of certainty and a sense of belief. It provides a sense of purpose and significance to the work of the school and all its members of staff. In these schools, devolvement of tasks and empowerment of members of staff are more effective in that decisions will have greater consistency because of the shared culture.

Understanding the culture of an organisation is being able to answer questions such as:

- What values do people in this organisation hold and operate by?
- How are people expected to treat each other?
- What motivates people?
- How are people judged and rewarded?
- Where does authority lie?
- How are decisions made?
- What is the approved style of doing things?

TEAM OBJECTIVES

The aims or the vision of the school, department or team, no matter how good they may seem, are merely empty rhetoric unless they are translated into action. It is the development of objectives that ensures the effectiveness of this translation as objectives, being much more specific, should be measurable, either through quantified means or by applying a professional judgement (e.g. assessment of the quality of teaching during lesson observations).

Objectives are short term, are school or team specific and are much more likely to be modified in light of school/department priorities and the needs of the pupils. They are framed such that they can be judged against the performance indicators or success criteria set. Some will be easy to quantify (e.g. test and examination results), whilst others (e.g. changes in pupil attitude or motivation) will require some form of professional judgement. Because of this, objectives should always include reference to the action to be taken. They should not simply be more specific aims. Some schools and teams use the terms 'aims' and 'objectives' as though they were synonymous; instead, it may be easier and more appropriate to refer to 'aims/vision' and 'intended outcomes', which implies action and the aspect of measurability or judgement. As objectives require action it is important to understand that, whilst all areas of the work of the team need to have objectives, it is not realistic to be working actively on more than a few at a time. Ideally, the objectives become 'internalised' by all members of the team. As with the formulation of aims, it is vital that all staff contribute to the development of objectives, take ownership of them and therefore ease the internal standardisation when measures or judgements are made.

The aims and intended outcomes of the teams/subjects are invariably used in school documents such as the school brochure and, more often, in option booklets for pupils in Year 9 and in Year 11 for those intending to enter sixth forms.

TEAM POLICIES

The introduction of OFSTED inspections of schools, in 1993, led to a proliferation of written policies, by schools, departments/teams and for subjects, where previously few or none had existed. This was, in one way, a good development as it required at least some thought on the procedures which had, in the main, simply been a part of the custom and practice of some schools/teams. The early evidence from OFSTED inspections, however, was critical about the process through which these policies had been developed. Subsequently, development planning has improved as a process, but there continues to be criticism, in inspection reports, about the stages of implementation, monitoring and evaluation within the planning process.

The valuable time spent on the development of well-thought-out, clearly documented policy statements or plans is largely wasted if these are not implemented, monitored and then evaluated to find out if the plans/policies have been effective in achieving the intended outcomes. Whilst there is value, of course, in the process of policy development, this is soon dissipated if there is no process of implementation, review and evaluation, i.e. policies into practice. All schools will have a range of policies in place. Many of these are statutorily required whereas others are optional but nonetheless desirable.

The obligatory policies are:

- admissions;
- the aims and objectives of the school (or Mission, Vision, Values);*
- appraisal (performance and pay review);*
- charging and remission of charges;*

- child protection;*
- curriculum, assessment/recording/reporting;*
- health and safety;*
- length of the school day;*
- pay;*
- pupil discipline;*
- religious education and collective worship;*
- sex education;*
- special educational needs;*
- staff competence;*
- staff discipline;
- staff grievance.

Other policies which the school is likely to have in place include:

- drug education;*
- equal opportunities;*
- multicultural issues;*
- redundancy;
- development plan;*
- staff development and in-service training;*
- examination entry.

Whilst some of these are essentially whole school policies, those marked with an asterisk should form a part of team and, in most cases, subject policies, although some are specific to particular subjects (e.g. religious education and sex education). In all instances, policies created by teams must concur with whole school policies and must not in any way contradict the issues covered by the school policies. This can be avoided if a member of the school management team is asked to approve or edit policies in draft or review form before they are finalised and then implemented.

The presentation, style and format of team documentation and/or a handbook are important if it is to fulfil the function of a working document for all staff, including temporary and supply teachers and teachers in training. The documentation must also be available and accessible to the headteacher, the governing body and OFSTED inspectors.

The handbook or documentation should be reviewed annually and, as parts of it may be subject to more regular review, it is recommended that it is in loose-leaf form. Colour coding of the various sections may also help to facilitate its use. It may be that, in some schools, there is an agreed policy for the format of all school handbooks which should therefore be followed.

DOCUMENTATION FOR OFSTED INSPECTIONS

All schools have now been through the first phase of the OFSTED inspection process and will be aware of the documentation that is required. Although most schools now provide full documentation, the criticisms of OFSTED inspectors often focused on three main issues relating to departmental/subject policies:

- Documentation had been developed without any apparent process, so much so that, in some instances, some members of teams seemed unaware of the policies; it is preferable, for OFSTED inspections, to submit outline or draft copies of incomplete policies, rather than to pretend that all policies have been fully developed and implemented;
- Where policies had been adequately developed, there was little evidence of their being implemented, i.e. the inspectors found no evidence of 'policies into practice';
- There was little evidence of effective evaluation of the policies that had been implemented; there seemed to be a reliance on the 'feel good factor' rather than on any measurable or professional judgemental evidence.

In addition to this, there was often insufficient use made of the oral feedback by inspectors to schools on the departmental/subject reports at the end of the period of inspection. Such an important, lengthy and somewhat less formal evaluation of the work of the team should be the focus of future team meetings in order to interpret what would appear, in a much shortened, more formal written version, in the full OFSTED report on the school. In some instances, there was also insufficient use of the inspectors' feedback to the school management team at this stage. While the report is still in a preliminary, draft form, suggestions for amendments might be made by the school so that the much shorter departmental/subject reports, within the full report, better reflect the true worth and work of the departments/teams.

As planning for subsequent inspections takes place, there is a clear need to consider those issues which were highlighted by the inspectors alongside the existing priorities in the team's development plan. Just as the governors have to produce an action plan, the team should produce an action plan for the issues raised at team level, but not to the exclusion of other development issues that the team might have already identified as priorities. There still remains the need to prioritise the development work of the team, except in those instances where the inspectors found evidence of non-compliance with statutory requirements (e.g. with respect to the National Curriculum or assessment, or on health and safety issues). *Supplement P1* provides one example of the approach that might be used for action planning including a suggested proforma to use as a working document.

Leadership and Management Areas

The areas of leadership and management, many requiring policy formulation and implementation, are listed under the following headings:

1 Curriculum and assessment management;
2 Staff management;
3 Pupil management;
4 Resource management;
5 Information and communications technology (ICT) in teaching, organisation, management and administration;
6 Financial management;
7 Routine administrative procedures.

This is the usual sort of list produced when the roles and responsibilities of middle managers are presented, in that these cover the professional tasks, skills and attributes required in order to perform effectively. However, three other aspects of management, at all levels in schools, underpin them:

- Management of time (*Supplement M1*)
- Recognition and management of stress in self and others (*Supplements M2* and *S4*);
- Management of conflict (*Supplements M2* and *M4*; see also Staff management, Pupil management).

All of these have become important issues and are regularly commented on by teachers' professional associations. The latter two fall into the category of 'people' or personnel skills and responsibilities and are often given too little prominence in the guidance documents emanating from central government.

1 CURRICULUM AND ASSESSMENT MANAGEMENT
(Supplement CA1)

In reviewing any aspect of the team's curriculum policy, the audit approach illustrated in *Supplements P9* and *CA1* should be of value. As a team exercise, this process should ensure that all staff are aware of the existing policy documentation and procedures that are already complete and implemented and others that are in need of review or further development.

Curriculum Content

There should be a broad statement which identifies all the relevant elements of the National Curriculum in the appropriate Key Stages and for post-16 work where there is post-statutory provision. In addition, the statement should include all issues relating to the delivery of any cross-curricular skills, particularly literacy, numeracy and ICT capability (see *Supplement CA6*).

The National Curriculum Subject Orders contain:

- Common Requirements;
- Programmes of Study;
- Attainment Targets;
- Level Descriptions.

In addition, the Orders for English and PE contain some General Requirements highlighting specific issues relating to these subjects.

Common Requirements

These stress the importance of access to the curriculum for all pupils and of making appropriate provision for pupils who have visual, sensory or physical impairment. There is also specific reference to the 'Use of Language' including each subject's contribution to the development and proficiency in the use of language. There is provision, in principle, in regard to Information and Communications Technology and the way in which subjects (with the exception of PE) can contribute to pupils' ICT capability.

Programmes of Study

These constitute the minimum statutory entitlement for pupils covering the knowledge, skills and understanding for each subject at each Key Stage. They provide the foundation which teachers must use in their planning of learning and teaching, in the formulation of schemes of work and in the day-to-day assessment of pupils' progress.

Attainment Targets

As the name implies, these define the standards of performance/achievement expected of the majority of pupils at the end of the Key Stage in terms of a level of achievement (on a scale of 1 to 8) or by an End of Key Stage Description.

Level Descriptions

These replace the statements of attainment used in the original National Curriculum and describe what pupils can or should be able to understand and do. They are designed to ensure that progression within each subject is clear and that levels across subjects are comparable. Teachers should judge which description 'best fits' the standard of achievement of each pupil against the attainment target(s). At the end of Key Stages 1–3, for all subjects except art, music and physical education, standards of pupils' performance are set out in eight level descriptions of increasing difficulty, with an additional description above level 8 to help teachers to differentiate and recognise 'exceptional performance'. An example of a level description is:

> *Mathematics – Attainment Target 2: Number and Algebra – Level 2*
> Pupils count sets of objects reliably, and use mental recall of addition and subtraction facts to 10. They have begun to understand the place value of each digit in a number and use this to order numbers up to 100. They choose the appropriate operation when solving addition and subtraction problems. They identify and use halves and quarters, such as half of a rectangle or a quarter of eight objects. They recognise sequences of numbers, including odd and even numbers.
>
> (DES Circular 5/89)

For art, music and physical education, End of Key Stage Descriptions set out the standard of performance expected of the majority of pupils at the end of each Key Stage. Descriptions of 'exceptional performance' are also provided in art and music at the end of Key Stage 3 and in physical education at the end of Key Stages 3 and 4. An example of an End of Key Stage Description is:

> *Physical Education – Key Stage 3*
> Pupils devise strategies and tactics for appropriate activities and plan or compose more complex sequence of movements. They adapt and refine existing skills and apply these to new situations. They show that they can use skills with precision and perform sequences with greater clarity and fluency. Pupils recognise the importance of rules and apply them. They appreciate strengths and limitations in performance and use this information in co-operative team work as well as to outwit the opposition in competition. They understand the short-term and long-term effects of exercise on the body systems, and demonstrate how to prepare for particular activities and how to recover after vigorous physical activity.
>
> (DES Circular 5/89)

Curriculum Organisation

Schemes of Work (Supplement CA2)

The comments in the OFSTED (1998) review of secondary schools in England, 1993–97, were positive in identifying that schemes of work are much improved. However, the continuity of curriculum planning between primary and secondary schools is not given sufficient priority in many secondary schools.

The schemes are the most obvious working documents for the teachers in each subject or year group and, whilst they will form a part of the departmental or subject handbook, there needs to be a separate copy for teachers to use as a part of their day-to-day teaching materials along with more detailed lesson plans (see below).

Schemes need to be specific, without constraining the professional expertise of the individual teacher. They are usually organised on a term-by-term basis but some teams prefer a more detailed breakdown on a weekly basis.

In secondary schools some departments still rely on Examination Board syllabuses as schemes of work for Years 10 and 11 and for the sixth form. It is important to realise that 'syllabuses' (including National Curriculum Programmes of Study) are essentially lists of content to be covered; they are not designed as schemes of work and therefore need to be translated into working documents to include issues such as suggested methodologies, resources and assessment opportunities.

The scheme(s) should contain information relating to the following:

- the rationale (the mission) for the area/topic being covered;
- evidence of how the National Curriculum programmes and/or examination syllabuses are being covered;
- suggested teaching strategies and methodologies (*Supplement TL5*);
- learning strategies (*Supplements TL2–4*);
- learning and teaching resources available/needed;
- differentiation strategies (by task and outcome), including reinforcement and extension work;
- evidence of progression and continuity;
- cross-curricular elements (*Supplement CA6*);
- homework;
- assessment strategies;
- time allocations.

In addition, schemes of work will be inspected for:

- coverage of the National Curriculum and examination syllabuses;
- differentiation strategies;
- provision of practical ideas, tasks and activities;
- evidence of activities which support the learning of specific competencies;
- provision of opportunities for pupils to progress to higher levels;
- suggestions for assessment opportunities;
- criteria to judge success (performance indicators).

Lesson Plans

Although many teachers rely on schemes of work as lesson plans, there is clearly an advantage in having more detailed approaches, particularly where work is planned within greater time constraints. In addition, the introduction of new courses or syllabuses is always an opportunity to plan in this amount of detail in the first instance. For experienced teachers, the level of detail required for use in specific lessons may be minimal but if a course or topic is planned in this detail it is invaluable for teachers acting as cover for absent colleagues, new staff, temporary and supply teachers, and teachers on teaching practice.

Lesson plans should indicate:

- activities – the types of activity and the sequence in which they are to be carried out, giving an indication of the timescale allowed and, where appropriate, the means by which pupils will move from one activity to another;
- teaching approaches – suggestions for the variety of methods to be used;
- key questions – to be asked at critical points;
- resources – stimulus materials, activity sheets, equipment, etc.;
- differentiation – provision of alternative materials to allow for variety in both task and outcome for the most and least able pupils (see Special Educational Needs, pp. 51–2);
- anticipated learning outcomes;
- organisation of pupils – variety in the use of whole class, group, paired and individual work;
- assessment – critical points need to be identified for the variety and use of assessment opportunities;
- success criteria – individual lessons should have identified success criteria in order to give some indication of anticipated learning gain, even if this is of a limited or speculative nature.

Homework

The OFSTED (1998) review of secondary schools recognised the great potential of homework for raising standards but commented that it continues to be a weakness in many schools. While some teachers take great care to set appropriately challenging homework on a regular basis, all too often homework fails to enthuse or challenge pupils as it might.

A clear statement is required of the policy relating to homework, again in line with any whole school policy. This should identify the timing and the quantity to be set and the procedures for collection, marking and return to pupils.

The DfEE has produced guidance on all aspects of homework in a booklet, *Homework: Guidelines for Primary and Secondary Schools* (1998). A recommended length of time is given for homework in each of the year groups together with some suggested topics (see Table 1).

The times are, of course, more manageable in Key Stages 1 and 2 where pupils are very largely class based rather than subject/department based. There is a need in Key Stages 3 and 4 for co-ordination across subjects to meet these recommendations (see also Schemes of Work, pp. 25–6).

Equal Opportunities

There should be a statement of the team's approach to access to the subject for all pupils and any special features relating to the nature of the subject. This statement should include issues of gender, ethnicity and special educational needs, especially those relating to ability, in particular linguistic needs.

The OFSTED (1998) review of secondary schools identified as a matter of serious concern aspects of under-performance within the following areas of equal opportunities:

Table 1 Guidelines for homework, years 1 to 13+

Year Groups	Recommended Time	Topics/Subjects
1 and 2	1 hour/week (1.07 and 1.19)*	Reading, spelling, other literacy work and number work
3 and 4	1.5 hours/week (1.36 and 1.43)*	Literacy and numeracy as for Years 1 and 2 with occasional assignments in other subjects
5 and 6	30 minutes/day (2.07 and 2.26)*	Regular weekly schedule with continued emphasis on literacy and numeracy but also ranging widely over the curriculum
7 and 8	45–90 minutes/day (5h 39m to 6h 27m per week)*	Timetabled programme across the subjects in curriculum
9	1–2 hours/day (7h 42m per week)*	Timetabled across the subjects of the curriculum
10 and 11	1.5–2.5 hours/day (10h 12m to 10h 32m per week)*	Timetabled according to the programmes leading to examination entry including course-work where appropriate
12 and 13	Governed by individual programmes of work	Determined by subjects being studied and taking into account time available for private study in school hours

* Average figures (in hours and minutes per week) arising from an OFSTED telephone survey, in which headteachers were asked how much homework was set in terms of the estimated amount of time required.

Source: Homework: Guidelines for Primary and Secondary Schools (DfEE 1998).

- boys;
- pupils from some ethnic minority groups;
- the wide gap between the highest and lowest attaining pupils (which has continued to increase since 1991).

Whilst all teachers need to be familiar with the Code of Practice relating to pupils with special educational needs (SEN), it is advantageous for a member of the team to have specific responsibility for the co-ordination of SEN issues. Alternatively, maximum use should be made of a member of staff in the school who has this expertise, usually the school's Special Education Needs Co-ordinator (SENCO).

Extra-curricular Activities

OFSTED evidence has shown that extra-curricular provision continues to be good or better in four out of five secondary schools. There is a variety of provision which adds to the overall benefit for the pupils through the goodwill of teachers who are prepared to give of their own time. A growing area is the use of this time to provide an extension to the curriculum, e.g homework clubs, time before and after school for work on additional subjects.

Many schools use extra-curricular time to foster pupils' physical, personal, social and cultural development through sport, drama, music and travel, all of which also encourage the 'team approach'. These activities are particularly effective where they encourage parental and community involvement.

Some schools have used the time effectively for the extension of the more able pupils, providing an enrichment to their studies and experience of the world of work and higher education institutions. Exhibitions, debates, competitions and large-scale technology projects have been particularly effective in providing a broader view of the subject and its value within the adult world.

Assessment, Recording and Reporting

Although the general pattern of assessment and reporting remains the same, the detailed requirements are likely to change with some frequency and so it is always necessary to check the current regulations by referring to the QCA/DfEE booklet, *Assessment and Reporting Arrangements*, which is normally produced in November each year. Sufficient copies of each of the Key Stages booklets are sent directly to schools for distribution to all heads of department/subject, all teachers of English, mathematics and science and the teachers responsible for pupils in classes at the end of Key Stages 1 and 2, as well as reception classes in primary schools. It is important, however, that all teachers are made aware of the contents of the booklet, particularly the reporting requirements. Heads of departments/subjects and curriculum co-ordinators have a responsibility to ensure that all teachers of the subjects are aware of both the assessment and reporting requirements. Further copies of the booklet can be obtained, free of charge, from QCA Publications or may be downloaded from QCA's website (see p. 200).

The booklet contains all elements of the statutory requirements as well as information and guidance on the processes and timetables involved. The regulations apply to all maintained schools and to those independent schools who decide to participate in the national assessment and reporting arrangements.

Assessment

Teachers have a contractual duty to:

- administer the national assessment arrangements;
- identify, for assessment purposes, all pupils who are in the final year of their Key Stage;
- provide teacher assessment levels and, from these, the overall subject level;
- ensure that all pupils in their final year of Key Stage 3 are assessed, including those older and younger pupils who are due to begin Key Stage 4 Programmes of Study the following year; a check should be made of the regulations concerning absence, lateness, illness, disapplication from and modification of the assessment.

In addition, middle managers may have a direct involvement in the duty of headteachers to:

- ensure security and confidentiality of the test materials for Key Stages 1, 2 and 3;
- comply with the arrangements for external marking, national data collection and reporting to parents;

- arrange for Key Stage 1 pupils, who are capable of achieving level 4 or above in mathematics and/or English, to take the appropriate Key Stage 2 tests.

LEA and QCA officers may make unannounced visits to a sample of schools before, during and after the test period to check that the correct security arrangements are being followed. Security and invigilation are expected to be of the same standard as required by examination boards for public examinations.

Schools will receive notification of test results by the end of June. These will be sent separately from the return of marked scripts. Any requests for reviews of marking need to be submitted by mid-July. Schools will be notified of the outcome of the reviews by the end of September. The precise dates will be announced annually.

There is also a statutory requirement to gather and record evidence of pupils' attainment from:

- observations of practical and oral work;
- written work completed in class;
- homework;
- school assessments, tests and examinations.

This should give an all round judgement of the level that a pupil has achieved in each attainment target. The records must be updated at least once a year.

The form of records and the amount of evidence is not statutorily prescribed but should identify the level of knowledge, skills and understanding displayed by each pupil. However, the system and procedures used by the team should ensure consistency of the standards and there should be evidence of agreed interpretations of these standards through internal moderation procedures. National Curriculum assessment, recording and reporting systems are subject to inspection by OFSTED.

There are further statutory requirements on the arrangements for reporting to parents (*Supplement CA5*) which apply to the whole school. It may be that a copy of the school's policy, or an extract from it, should be included in each team's documentation, particularly the timetable of events through the assessment and reporting process.

Test and examination entry

Although the school may have a policy relating to the entry of pupils for tests and examinations, guidance should also be provided on the process of decision making on entry, and the reasons for or against, and the way in which pupils and their parents are involved and informed. In secondary schools, liaison with the school's examination officer is vital to ensure that appropriate and accurate information is given and recorded.

The examination entry policy, relating to both tests and examinations and the tier of entry, where this applies, should take account of the needs as well as the abilities of the pupils. This should also be made explicit to the parents before final decisions are made. The introduction of tiered papers in many subjects has created a two-level decision, i.e. whether to enter and if so for which tier. There is a tendency to be pressured to enter the higher tier but the experience of examination boards is that borderline candidates do better in intermediate or foundation level papers. This often needs careful explanation to most parents.

Care should be taken in considering some of the published analyses of the 'ease' or 'difficulty' of different Boards' syllabuses for both GCSE and A level examinations. Some of these analyses are based on the erroneous belief that the ranges of abilities of the pupils being entered for the different Boards' examinations are the same. It is important to consider the range of abilities in each Board's entry as some tend to serve more restricted ranges of schools (e.g. more entries from public and independent schools than from comprehensive schools).

At the end of Key Stage 4 pupils will be assessed through GCSE or a recognised equivalent organised by an accredited examination board or other body (e.g. the Business and Technology Education Council, the Royal Society of Arts, the City and Guilds of London Institute). However, the moves by central government to reduce the number of Examination Agencies to three across England and Wales should rationalise the provision over the next few years. All examinations or assessment procedures must have statutory approval and lists of these are produced annually. Although schools have to teach the programmes of study for the statutory subjects of the National Curriculum, there is no requirement for schools to enter pupils for examinations. However, the schools charging policy will make reference to the parents' rights to pay for the entry. Pupils not entered for public examination may have their performance and/or progress measured exclusively by teachers' assessment and the outcomes recorded in their National Record of Achievement.

Target setting, benchmarking and value added (Supplements CA3 and CA4)

From 1 September 1998, schools have been required to set targets in relation to the performance of pupils in National Curriculum assessments and public examinations. In primary schools, this also involved a baseline assessment for all pupils entering the school, including entry to reception classes attached to the school. The QCA has produced a range of accredited schemes and a list of these can be obtained from the Early Years Team (see p. 200). Funding is available for training, to purchase assessment materials and to provide supply cover to support the administration of baseline assessment schemes.

The statutory requirement for schools to set annual targets in relation to the performance of pupils aged 11, in the end of Key Stage 2 National Curriculum assessments, and pupils aged 16 in public examinations came into effect in September 1998. Governing bodies are responsible for setting and publishing targets by 31 December each year. DfEE Circular 11/98 provides practical guidelines and detailed information about the publication and targets setting timetable, although schools may set additional targets. To support further the target setting process, QCA, DfEE and OFSTED publish a package of performance data during each autumn term. The package contains a summary of national results, benchmarking and value added analyses. The benchmarking data provide schools with information about the performance of other schools with similar characteristics to their own against which they can compare their own performance.

The QCA published the first pamphlet containing this information early in 1998. The information was based on data from a large sample of schools in 1997 and the benchmarking used was the proportion of pupils, in the whole school, known to be eligible for free school meals (FSM) and whether the school was selective or not. The national data which were provided identified schools in six bands, i.e. up to 5%,

6–9%,10–13%,14–21%, 22–35% and more than 35% eligibility for FSM. Schools are able, therefore, to identify the band in which they would fall.

The statutory target setting will apply to pupils' performance in the year 2000, and each year thereafter, based on:

- at the end of Key Stage 2 (11 year olds):
  – the percentage of registered pupils who (it is anticipated) will *in the following year* be in the final year of KS2 and will achieve:

    – level 4 or above in the NC tests in English;
    – level 4 or above in the NC tests in mathematics;

- at the end of Key Stage 4 (16 year olds):
  – the percentage of registered pupils in the relevant age group who (it is anticipated) will *by the end following school year* achieve:

    – 5 or more GCSE Grades A*–C;
    – 1 or more Grades A*–G;

  (In both cases these percentages should include equivalent vocational qualifications or a combination of both)

    – the average point score for the school in GCSE and vocational qualifications.

In both Key Stages, the percentages are also given in 'bands':

- 95 percentile – performance exceeded by 5% of schools;
- Upper quartile – performance exceeded by 25% of schools;
- Median – performance exceeded by 50% of schools;
- Lower quartile – performance below which 25% of schools fall.

Schools are therefore able to compare their results with the national data and so more accurately compare their performance with similar schools with similar free school meals eligibility.

The QCA also provided national data for the end of Key Stages 3 and 4 assessments in grammar schools and secondary modern schools. This adds, in an overall way, some benchmarking data based on prior ability measures.

The value added analyses compare the performance of nationally representative samples of pupils at the end of Key Stages 2 and 3 and at GCSE/GNVQ against their prior attainment at Key Stages 1, 2 and 3 respectively. These analyses will enable schools to compare the progress of their pupils with the average progress of pupils nationally who began the Key Stage with the same prior attainment.

LINKS TO THE NATIONAL LITERACY AND NUMERACY TARGETS
The statutory KS2 school targets are based on the same measures as the national literacy and numeracy targets for 2002. The literacy targets have already been agreed by the DfEE with LEAs and in due course the numeracy targets will be agreed. Part of the role of the LEAs is to ensure that targets set by individual schools will collectively add up to the LEA's overall targets.

ADDITIONAL (NON-STATUTORY) SCHOOL TARGETS
Schools, without reference to the LEA, may set additional targets, taking into consideration how these might be effective in supporting school improvement. Such targets may be relevant to:

- pupils with SEN – where there is a high proportion of such pupils, targets relating to percentages attaining levels 1, 2 and 3 in English and mathematics might be published;
- high ability pupils – targets relating to higher NC levels might be appropriate and relevant.

THE ROLE OF THE LEA
The LEAs will have an important role in:

- helping schools to set realistic and challenging targets;
- supporting schools in the process of analysis and disseminating performance data;
- agreeing with schools the LEA targets for inclusion in their Educational Development Plans (EDPs).

The QCA is continuing to consult with schools and LEAs about both target setting and benchmarking and intends to include further information on pupils' prior attainment for benchmarking purposes. However, it is expected that LEAs will use the national data as a starting point for more detailed local analyses to help the target setting process in their schools.

Reference should be made to the pamphlet *Benchmark Information for Key Stages 3 and 4* published annually by QCA. The DfEE has also published a guidance booklet, *From Targets to Action* (1997), on the setting of challenging targets

Marking
The OFSTED (1998) review of secondary schools made the following comment on marking:

> the marking of pupils' work often fails to make the best use of pupils' responses in order to comment on the strengths and weaknesses and promote improvement. In general, assessment is one of the weaker aspects of teaching.

Across the team there needs to be an agreed and consistent approach to the form of marking of pupils' work. Marking needs to be constructive, diagnostic and easily understood by the pupils and parents in order to enable them to better judge the strengths and weaknesses in the work and progress.

Recording

Achievement data on pupils
Although the school will maintain much detailed information on pupils, it is important that teams keep their own more specific achievement data. However, there is little point in duplicating the data held centrally by the school as long as the specific data required by the department are easily and readily accessible.

If progress of pupils is to be monitored, data on achievement at the time of entry to the school are vital. For some areas the achievement data at pre-school and Key Stage 2 are available, but for areas outside the existing Key Stage 2 testing arrangements, any achievement data, particularly standardised data, are useful in providing a baseline measure of achievement (benchmarking) against which future attainment/achievement can be measured and compared. Similarly, results of any internal standardised tests and results at Key Stages 1 and 3 enable progress in achievement for individual pupils to be measured as they progress through the school.

In secondary schools, Key Stage 3 data can, in part, be used to predict performance at 16+, as well as for targeting purposes, and should be used to guide examination entry, particularly where there are tiered papers for GCSE. Departments should also use results to measure 'value-added' in 16+ examinations at subject level, alongside whole school data. Where appropriate, a similar approach should be used with results at 16+ and the entry and performance of pupils at 18+.

If such data are not already available, it is important to begin to collect the information as soon as possible if longitudinal studies of pupil performance are to be used as one means of improving pupil performance (*Supplement CA4*).

Reporting *(Supplement CA5)*

Schools are required to report to parents annually on each pupil. The report goes to the parents of pupils under 18, and to the pupils themselves if over that age. The report can be sent by post or 'pupil post'. The report must give information showing the pupil's educational achievements in relation to the relevant Key Stage as indicated above.

The reporting requirements vary according to the age and stage of the pupils as well as the destinations of the reports and the details of each of these is given in *Supplement CA5* under the following headings:

- Reception to Year 2;
- Key Stage 2: Years 3–6;
- Key Stage 3: Years 7–9;
- Key Stage 4 and beyond: Years 10 and 11, and 12, 13 and 14+;
- Reports to school leavers;
- Additional reporting information;
- Reports to receiving schools;
- The headteacher's role in reporting.

Although the general pattern is not likely to change, the detailed requirements may be varied, possibly each year, and it is necessary to check the current regulations by referring to the latest QCA/DfEE pamphlets, *Assessment and Reporting Arrangements*. These are published for the four Key Stages and copies are sent directly to schools.

2 STAFF MANAGEMENT

Job Descriptions *(Supplement S6)*

Details of teaching and support staff should be recorded, indicating their roles and responsibilities as well as their particular strengths and areas of expertise. Agreed job descriptions provide a valuable aid in many ways. Often these are regarded as a 'straitjacket' of responsibilities but, used effectively, they can provide a useful guide to professional development and can allow much more accurate and authoritative references on staff to be written. They should not be seen as fixed descriptions and a review at least annually is valuable if they are to aid professional involvement and development of the staff.

Job descriptions linked to the appointment of staff are somewhat different and are outlined on pp. 40–1.

Monitoring of Learning and Teaching *(Supplements TL1 and TL2)*

Although there is a statutory requirement for a school teacher appraisal system, in many instances this may not have fulfilled the original intention or been as effective as was expected when it was introduced. If the element of monitoring and evaluation of learning and teaching is to be effective, a much more rigorous approach to classroom observation and professional feedback needs to be in place. Even without a school policy, teams would benefit from the establishment of an agreed system for a positive, professional approach to classroom observation, evaluation and feedback. This is often difficult to achieve as there may be a reluctance to 'invade' the professionalism of colleagues. However, many schools are increasingly coming to use this approach as a means of sharing and disseminating good practice and thereby improving the quality of effective teaching across the department/team, with the consequent improvement in the quality of learning and the raising of the standards of pupil achievement.

A description of the process, the criteria and the associated proformas, all based in part on the OFSTED procedures, are given in *Supplement TL1*.

In the monitoring and evaluation process, care should be taken to ensure that the varieties of pupils' learning and the different styles of teaching are all considered. These aspects of teaching and learning are fully discussed in *Supplements TL2–TL5*. Many teachers have quite individualistic styles of teaching, perhaps not as easily categorised as suggested in these Supplements. Nonetheless, what needs to be judged is the effectiveness of the teaching in relation to the increase in learning gain by the pupils. There is always a danger that the observer will see any style different from his/her own as less effective. This is the critical element of professional honesty and acceptance. The use of an in-service training exercise, such as that based on Kolb's (1984) work which is described in *Supplement TL3*, can be a useful precursor to introducing a team, or school, process for the monitoring and evaluation of teaching and learning.

Professional Development *(Supplements P4 and S2)*

Records of each teacher's professional development should be maintained. Details of attendance at conferences, courses, workshops, and so on, provide a valuable record of the professional approach taken by the team to its own development. Similarly, some record should be kept of 'internal' activities for individual staff and of sessions which have been held for the whole team/department. OFSTED inspectors will want to see evidence of such training and will want to assess, wherever they can, any impact that this has had on the overall performance of the department/team.

As most professional development initiatives are costly, in terms of time and/or finance, it is important that a 'needs identification' process is undertaken initially. This should be linked to the plans that the team/department have made or intend to pursue, and the planning process should help to identify any gaps in the experience or expertise of individuals or the team as a whole. The school teacher appraisal (performance review) should also provide useful evidence of training and development needs. As most schools have a 'senior' member of staff with responsibility for professional development it is important that this person is kept informed of any priority needs that are identified. As finance for training and development is likely to be scarce, resources must be allocated as economically and effectively as possible amongst team members.

One of the major difficulties following any in-service training is the dissemination of the development to other members of the team. This is relatively easy where the activity has entailed purely information gathering but activities involving experiential learning are much more difficult to pass on to colleagues. Another difficulty is the process of evaluation of the impact of any in-service training on the work of the team and, because it might be much longer term, the effects on the quality of teaching and learning. Nonetheless, every effort should be made to keep this evaluation to the fore, bearing in mind the cost and effort involved in the training.

Much valuable professional development can be done within the team, which helps to overcome the difficulties of dissemination and evaluation. In addition, the rotation of teaching programmes and the sharing of team responsibilities through delegation help in professional development. However, in some schools, delegation has often been more a case of shedding jobs than the more positive approach that in modern management terms is usually described as empowerment. This process is covered in *Supplement S1* and is a much more positive attempt to enable members of the team to share responsibility while allowing the middle manager to concentrate on his/her leadership and management functions. This will provide all with the opportunity for professional growth and development as well as engendering the feeling of some ownership of the work of the team.

When considering staff development, care should be taken to include the needs of any support staff associated with the team. If they are truly regarded as members of the team, and are supporting the work of teaching and learning, their needs may, in some instances, be more important on specific issues. The funding arrangements for in-service training have been somewhat relaxed in order for such training to be funded from GEST allocations.

The previous Conservative government produced, through the Teacher Training Agency, a framework for the professional development of teachers (*Supplement S2*). It seems that the present government intends to follow a similar path in the Schools Standards and Framework Bill with a commitment to 'substantially increased funding for training'.

Appraisal, Performance, Expectations and Standards

Teaching Staff

The existing appraisal scheme

At present there is a statutory obligation to carry out appraisal, on a two-year repeating cycle, of every teacher employed in maintained schools, other than those teachers working less than 40 per cent of full time. However, in some schools all part-time teachers have opted to be involved in the appraisal process. The purpose of appraisal is to assist school teachers in their professional development and career planning, and to promote the quality of education by enabling teachers to carry out their duties more effectively.

Appraisal may not be used as a disciplinary sanction and it has the following specific objectives:

- to recognise the achievements of teachers and to help them to identify ways of improving their skills and performance;
- to assist teachers, the governing body and (where relevant) the LEA in determining whether a change of duties would help professional development and career prospects;
- to identify potential for career development, supported by in-service training;
- to assist those teachers experiencing difficulties by offering support, guidance, training and/or counselling;
- to update existing job descriptions;
- to inform those responsible for providing references;
- to improve the management of schools.

Appraisals, other than those of headteachers, are carried out by teaching staff, which usually means the line manager within the school. There are compulsory elements of teacher appraisals:

- classroom observation;
- an appraisal interview;
- preparation of an appraisal statement;
- a formal review meeting.

It should be noted that the classroom observation element contrasts with that which is suggested, on p. 35, on monitoring and evaluating learning and teaching. Although the purposes are in some ways similar (e.g. to improve skills and performance), appraisal does not usually involve the much more detailed feedback element or the action plan for development/improvement.

Although individual appraisal outcomes are not reported to governors, collective targets that result from appraisals will be reported to the governing body and usually to the in-service training co-ordinators of the school and the LEA in order to identify priority needs for training programmes.

Relevant information from teacher appraisals may form a part of the Teacher's Annual Review whereby each teacher must be given a formal statement of his/her salary and how it has been determined. This is still subject to review as the present government seeks to include performance-related pay into a revised management review scheme.

In addition, an issue which might arise from appraisal is whether or not a teacher is competent, although this would normally stem from other contexts, such as parental and/or pupil complaints or the outcome of the more rigorous monitoring and evaluation of teaching and learning mentioned on p. 35.

The proposed appraisal scheme

In the present government's Schools Standards and Framework Bill the current teacher appraisal system is to be revised and linked to target setting for pupils' performance by individual teachers and headteachers. The reasons given are that whilst there are some strengths in the present system there are also some weaknesses.

The strengths of the present system are seen as:

- Teachers have found the appraisal process helpful, welcoming recognition of their achievements as well as constructive criticism and the opportunity to consider their professional development;
- The anxieties about classroom observation proved largely unfounded and the emphasis on teaching and learning was appreciated;
- Appraisers reported that they benefited from observing others teach.

However, weaknesses are seen as:

- The current arrangements are not sufficiently linked to policies for school and departmental management, including in-service training and development planning; this has been exacerbated by the misunderstanding of the confidentiality requirements and by the two-year cycle;
- Heads and teachers are looking for more rigorous target setting which, linked to improved planning for in-service training, could lead to better focused staff development and improved teaching;
- Evidence from OFSTED inspections found that only 20 per cent of schools visited showed discernible improvements in teaching following appraisals, and these were only minor ones;
- The bureaucracy tended to outweigh the benefits of appraisal; a closer integration of appraisal with other aspects of management could increase the impact on the quality of teaching whilst reducing the bureaucratic burden.

The new arrangements were to have come into effect in September 1999 once further consultation had taken place. However, the government published a Green Paper, *Teachers: Meeting the Challenge of Change*, in December 1998, which was much more radical and ambitious in its approach in an attempt to modernise the profession. It gave four priorities (principles) – better leadership, better rewards, better training and better support. Consultations took place between December and March 1999 and the new proposals are now due to come into effect in September 2000.

The key elements for teachers, other than headteachers and deputies, are:

- The proposals entail a significant strengthening of performance management in schools;
- The additional cash investment must lead to the establishment of proper systems for annual review and threshold assessment;
- A performance threshold will give access, by voluntary application, to a new higher range of pay for the most effective teachers as Advanced Skills Teachers (ASTs);

- Teachers will apply using a standard application form; clear criteria will be established and nationally trained, external assessors will work with heads to ensure fair and consistent judgements;
- The existing salary will continue for teachers who do not move to the new system and both scales will be kept under review by the Review body;
- Performance and pay review will be two distinct phases in performance management;
- Annual performance review will be part of the school's normal operating procedures; this will involve team leaders discussing and agreeing work and development priorities with each teacher in their team and will assess teachers' effectiveness and identify areas where there could be further development;
- The agreeing of personal objectives will be a school-based process carried out in the context of the school's development plan and any departmental or team plans; the purpose of the objectives will be to identify key priorities for teachers' work, including pupil progress, and the objectives may also include ways in which the teacher will contribute to team priorities and the teacher's own professional development;
- Monitoring will include a more formal discussion each year to review the teachers' effectiveness against the full range of their work; new research into characteristics of effective teaching will set a framework for assessment and for professional development;
- Annual reviews will identify competencies or subject areas on which teachers want to focus in order to develop their professional expertise; the reviews may well be used by teachers to build up a record of career and professional development to use for job applications, references and threshold applications;
- Decisions on pay and promotion will be informed by performance review; there are three distinct phases:

  - 'up to the performance threshold' – teachers can expect an annual increment if they are performing satisfactorily; double increments for exceptional performance would need to be justified by review outcomes. As at present, unsatisfactory overall performance may lead to the withholding of an increment;
  - 'threshold assessment' – this will be a separate process assessed against national criteria; annual reviews should help teachers to identify areas on which they need to focus to meet threshold standards and in time provide evidence needed for assessment;
  - 'teachers above the threshold, Advanced Skills Teachers and teachers in the leadership group' – these will have the opportunity of gaining higher salaries for sustained high quality performance;

- A draft Performance Management Framework is being developed to manage the system; this will set out the key elements of the new system, with minimum bureaucracy; model policies, based on existing good practice, will help schools to identify how they can build on their existing systems for planning, monitoring and appraisal;
- Substantial funds will be provided for support through the Standards Fund for professional development; this should give heads and teachers opportunities to use funding flexibly to meet national and school training priorities as well as teachers' individual needs;
- Aspects of the fast track were piloted from September 1999 to provide tailored training and support to excellent trainees and serving teachers and to allow both

to move rapidly through the new professional structure; it will also boost recruitment of the most highly talented to initial teacher training;

- The TTA has been asked to take forward work on developing numeracy tests for trainee teachers in the Summer of 2000 and tests in literacy and ICT for Summer 2001.

Non-Teaching Staff

There is no formal requirement that non-teaching staff undertake appraisal, although many schools, in the same way as good employers generally, will have appraisal or job review procedures for all staff. This is usually seen positively as a means of identifying job satisfaction and development needs and possibilities. It will often involve at least an annual review of the job description but the question of whether non-teaching staff meet expectations and required standards is a matter of the contractual terms of employment and, particularly, the job description.

Appointment and Induction of New Staff *(Supplement S6)*

Appointments

Middle managers are now much more likely to be directly involved in the appointment of both teaching and support staff to the team/department. It is therefore necessary to develop the skills involved in the appointments process. The appointment of staff represents the largest financial investment made by schools and so it is important to ensure that, in every case, the best possible appointment is made.

A summary of the stages in appointment include:

- a description of the post which, in the case of a replacement, may not be the same as that for the previous member of staff;
- a person specification, identifying the essential characteristics required of the applicants in order to supplement, and complement, those of the existing team;
- advertising the post;
- procedures for longlisting and/or shortlisting;
- confidential references;
- pre-interview visits;
- procedures for informal meetings, with appropriate staff, on the day of the interview;
- organisation of the interview;
- immediate post-interview induction.

Where a vacancy occurs, either through an increase in staffing or through a resignation, the process of appointment should begin as soon as possible in order to provide the maximum time to find the most appropriate person.

The stages in the appointment process include:

- The production of a description of the post which may not be the same as that for the previous member of staff, if any; a new appointment gives an opportunity to change the roles within the team and, through this, to encourage the further professional development of existing staff;

- A person specification, identifying the essential, and desirable, attributes required of the applicants in order to supplement and complement the character of the existing team; this might include attributes such as 'ability to work as a part of a team', 'to work under pressure and meet deadlines', 'to achieve challenging professional goals' but the exact demands will depend on the type and level of post being advertised;
- The advertisement for the post should be brief as there is a cost involved; the decision on where to place the advertisement will, in part, be determined by the nature of the post, e.g. an advert for a classroom assistant or technician would probably be better placed in the local/regional area than in the national press;
- Further details of the school and the subject/department should be prepared and should contain elements of the mission, vision and culture of the school/department/ team as well as further details of the job description;
- Procedures for shortlisting should be established before the application forms are received. The process might involve preliminary recommendations by the team/ department and decisions should be based on the criteria for the post sent out the potential applicants. Including too many candidates on a short-list for interview should be avoided. A maximum of five candidates should be chosen as any more will make the interviewing process long and less effective and will not enable full justice to be given to the candidates. Where it is felt necessary to produce a long-list for first interview, the additional costs, including time, must be borne in mind;
- Confidential references, from those persons identified by the candidates, should be taken up along with those from the candidates' present employers if not quoted by the candidates. The use of references in the interview process varies from school to school and LEA to LEA. Some use the references in longlisting or shortlisting, some during the interview decision-making process and others to confirm the appointment decision. The use of confidential references in shortlisting may delay the whole process as references may be slow in arriving. In addition, many LEAs may refuse to send a number of confidentials because of the extra work involved;
- In many instances arrangements are now made for a pre-interview visit of the shortlisted candidates, although this is often restricted to a visit in the morning of the day of the interviews. As interviews are two-way events, i.e. the school is making some judgement of the candidates and the candidates are making a judgement of the suitability of the school and the post, it is important that as much opportunity as possible is created for these two aspects;
- Increasingly interview procedures have come to include some form of presentation by the candidates to the interview panel. The title of a topic, which is relevant to the post, is sent to the candidates prior to the interview and they are asked to give a short talk on it. This allows judgements to be made on the candidates' ability to prepare in advance, their presentation skills, and their ability to be accurate and concise. It should be borne in mind that this creates additional pressure which some good candidates find difficult; if this approach is used it should be balanced against the other attributes that the candidates show in other parts of the appointment process;
- Another selection technique, used by some schools, is to ask candidates to teach a class for a short time, in order to test their classroom management skills. Their performance, of course, has to be judged in the light of their lack of knowledge of the pupils as well as the culture of the school. An alternative approach is to ask candidates to join a teacher with a class and to make comments on the lesson. These are also stressful situations for the candidates and careful thought needs to be given

to the process, including the information given to the candidates prior to the task, the choice of the group to be taught and the topic for presentation;

- Much other valuable information about the relative strengths, and shortcomings, of the candidates can be gained from the more informal contacts made, with as many staff as possible, during preliminary visits; there should be a mechanism for feeding this information into the formal interviews and decision making process;
- The middle manager may be asked to prepare, or be involved in the preparation of, topics for presentation by the candidates to the interview panel; in addition, requests may be made for prepared questions for the panel members to ask;
- The organisation of the interview may, in part, be pre-determined by the Articles of Government of the school, as may the selection of candidates for interview. Where middle managers are to be involved in the formal interviews, they will be expected to be the best prepared, since they have detailed knowledge of the demands of the post and some knowledge of the candidates already, having had longer to study and make judgements on the application forms;
- The role of the middle manager in the formal interview is as the 'technical expert', along with the LEA Inspector/Adviser, if appropriate; the questions asked by the middle manager should therefore be centred on the technical side of the job, allowing others to explore other features of the applicants' strengths and weaknesses;
- Interviews are stressful experiences for the candidates and interviewers need to be aware of the nervousness that candidates will show, particularly at the start of the interview. An air of casualness is often a normal cover-up for a feeling of nervousness. This nervousness may well cause some candidates to jabber or chatter, saying far more than they intended. It is important to put candidates at ease as quickly as possible if a true assessment of their candidature is to be made;
- Questions should be well prepared and should allow the candidates to exhibit their strengths; there should be no attempts to trap the candidates or to ask the 'clever' technical question. The best and most informative interviews are 'intensive conversations' rather than 'interrogations'. Questions requiring a simple 'yes' or 'no' answer should be avoided and, where used, should be simply to confirm points for clarification from the application form. It is important to get the candidate to talk and this is best done by asking 'open-ended' questions, e.g. 'can you tell us about your experience in/of . . .?';
- At the end of the interview, the role of the middle manager, whether involved in formal interviews or not, is to give the interview panel any other relevant information and insights that have come from the more informal contacts with the candidates prior to the interviews;
- Once the interviewing panel have made their decision and the formalities are concluded, the middle manager may be asked to recall the successful candidate and, possibly, to inform the unsuccessful ones of the decision. It is always better to wait until the successful candidate has been offered the post and has accepted before informing the unsuccessful ones. Increasingly, unsuccessful candidates, particularly for more 'senior' posts, ask for feedback on their interview performance. It is better to delay this until at least the following day as they may not be receptive to comments immediately after the disappointment of the interview decision;
- At the close of the interviews there should be a brief time to begin the process of induction of the successful candidate by, say, providing additional information and documentation, arranging for a further visit before taking up the post (see p. 43).

The process involved in the appointment of part-time, temporary or supply teachers and in the appointment of support staff may not be as formal or as intensive as described above. However, the process should follow the same pattern and the same care should be taken to ensure that the candidates can present their strengths and that areas of uncertainty in their candidature can be explored. Whilst the financial investment may not be as great in these appointments, the successful candidate will become part of the team and the work they will be expected to do may be just as important for the pupils' learning.

Induction of New Staff

The team should have policy and procedures for the induction of new staff which must complement and supplement the induction policy and procedures of the whole school, in line with the new regulations introduced in 1998 and 1999 (see below) for newly qualified teachers. Both school and team policies should have a rationale including the importance of valuing the work of all new staff. The induction process applies to all new appointments including full-time, part-time, temporary, supply and peripatetic teachers and support staff. The school policy should also include reference to other adults working in the school, e.g. clerical and administrative staff, caretakers, mid-day assistants. The policies should include reference to those responsible for the induction of each category of new staff. Obviously, the level of need will vary considerably but the guidance should include all essential items necessary for the particular teacher on a 'need to know' basis. A balance must be struck between trying to give too much detail and failing to provide enough for the new member of staff to make an effective start when taking up the post. The regulations with respect to newly qualified teachers are good examples of this.

For all newly appointed staff, preliminary visits are usual and much can be achieved through clear and up-to-date documentation. Similarly, for trainee teachers on teaching practice, the preliminary visit should be used to give this information and to prepare the teacher as fully as possible for the period of practice although the student teacher's needs, in terms of longer-term requirements, do not have to be as detailed.

Whilst all induction processes for new staff have features in common, the level of support needed will vary according to the nature of the post and the previous experience of the member of staff. However, all those new to the school will feel much more a part of the team, and of the whole school, if they are made to feel welcome and valued. The daily smile and enquiry on how things are going helps all newcomers (not least new pupils).

Newly Qualified Teachers (NQTs)

Reference should be made to the documents *National Standards for Qualified Teacher Status* (TTA 1998) and *Induction Requirements, Process and Procedures for Newly Qualified Teachers* (DfEE Circular 5/99; see p. 44). General points arising from the *National Standards* document include:

- All NQTs should be given the opportunity to demonstrate their proficiency in teaching classes of a size normal for the school and the subject(s) they are to teach;
- The following types of post are not generally suitable for NQTs:

  - those which present unusual problems of discipline or teaching techniques;

- supply teaching posts;
- peripatetic posts because of the lack of a stable setting for the development of teaching skills;

• Before taking up appointment the following should be made available to the NQT:

- a visit to the school to meet the school management team, head of the team/ department and other members of staff as appropriate;
- information in the form of relevant school and departmental/team documentation and/or handbooks;
- the teacher's timetable or at least some indication of the likely teaching commitments and any related curricular information, documentation and schemes of work;
- teaching resources which can be used to prepare at least the first series of lessons for each group that the NQT is to teach;
- information on, and a chance to see, other teaching resources, materials and equipment and the procedures for their use;
- information on the support and supervision for NQTs provided by the school and, if appropriate, the LEA;
- updates, e.g. staff bulletins; these are also useful for staff who are, or have been, on maternity leave or secondment;
- help and advice on personal issues, e.g. accommodation, finance;

• After taking up appointment the NQT should be able to:

- seek help and support from a nominated member of staff and the head of department or other appropriate member of staff;
- observe experienced colleagues teaching and to have opportunities to visit and observe teaching in other schools, wherever possible;
- have some of his/her teaching observed and evaluated by experienced colleagues and/or an LEA inspector/adviser and to receive prompt written, as well as oral, constructive feedback;
- become gradually involved in out of school activities, school working groups;
- have regular discussions and opportunities to share experiences with other NQTs by attending LEA or other meetings;
- receive praise, wherever possible, for things well done or indeed situations 'survived'.

From September 1998, newly trained teachers taking up posts in schools have had a Career Entry Profile and are expected to follow a structured training programme during their induction year, supported by a personal mentor. DfEE Circular 5/99 sets out guidance on how NQTs should be supported, monitored and assessed during the induction period. Any teachers obtaining QTS after 7 May 1999 have to complete an induction period of three school terms (or equivalent) within a period of five years. Details of the exceptions to this requirement are given in Circular 5/99 along with the problems associated with NQTs working on a part-time or supply basis.

The headteacher has responsibility for ensuring that the induction process and procedures are in place and for keeping the governing body informed. However, all middle managers in all schools with NQTs (including Curriculum Co-ordinators in primary schools) need to be involved in the process and therefore must be aware of the requirements listed below.

Key elements of the induction period for NQTs are as follows.

TEACHING TIMETABLES

NQTs will have a timetable of 90 per cent of the normal average teaching time (this will be written into subsequent School Teachers' Pay and Conditions Documents). In addition, this time must be protected as a part of a coherent induction programme and be distributed appropriately throughout the induction period.

STANDARDS

To meet the Induction Standards, NQTs should demonstrate that they:

- in planning, teaching and class management:

  - set clear targets for improvement of pupils' achievement, monitor pupils' progress towards those targets and use appropriate teaching strategies; including, where relevant, in relation to literacy, numeracy and other school targets;
  - plan effectively to ensure that pupils have the opportunity to meet their potential notwithstanding differences of race and gender, and taking into account the needs of pupils who are underachieving, very able or not yet fluent in English;
  - secure a good standard of pupil behaviour in the classroom through establishing appropriate rules and high expectations of discipline which pupils respect; acting to pre-empt and deal with inappropriate behaviour in the context of the behaviour policy of the school;
  - plan effectively, where applicable, to meet the needs of pupils with Special Educational Needs and, in collaboration with the SENCO, make an appropriate contribution to the preparation, implementation, monitoring and review of Individual Action Plans;
  - take account of ethnic and cultural diversity to enrich the curriculum and raise achievement;

- in monitoring, assessment, recording, reporting and accountability:

  - recognise the level that a pupil is achieving and make accurate assessments, independently, against attainment targets, where applicable, and performance levels associated with other tests or qualifications relevant to the subject(s) or phase(s) taught;
  - liaise effectively with pupils' parents/carers through informative oral and written reports on pupils' progress and achievements, discussing appropriate targets, and encouraging them to support their children's learning, behaviour and progress;

- in meeting other professional requirements:

  - where applicable, deploy support staff and other adults effectively in the classroom, involving them, where appropriate, in the planning and management of pupils' learning;
  - take responsibility for implementing school policies and practices, including those dealing with bullying and racial harassment;
  - take responsibility for their own professional development, setting objectives for improvements and taking action to keep up-to-date with research and developments in pedagogy and in the subject(s) they teach.

JOB DESCRIPTIONS *(Supplement S6)*
The NQT should not be given a job description that makes unreasonable demands.
All NQTs should normally serve the induction period in a post which:

- does not demand teaching outside the age range and subject(s) for which they have been trained;
- does not present them, on a day-to-day basis, with acute or especially demanding discipline problems;
- involves the regular teaching of the same class(es);
- involves similar planning, teaching and assessment processes to those in which teachers working in substantive posts in the school are engaged;
- does not involve additional non-teaching responsibilities without the provision of appropriate preparation and support.

OBSERVATION OF TEACHING AND FOLLOW-UP DISCUSSION

- The NQT should be observed teaching at least once in any six to eight week period, including in the first four weeks in post (in the case of part-time teachers the intervals should be adjusted accordingly);
- Observations should be based on particular aspects based on the NQT's objectives for development;
- The NQT and the observer should have a follow-up discussion to analyse the lessons observed;
- Observations and discussion should be agreed in advance and brief written record made on each occasion; the record should relate to the NQT's objectives and should indicate what action should be taken;
- While the tutor/mentor is likely to undertake most of the observations, other people from within or from outside the school may also be involved, e.g. teachers with particular specialisms or responsibilities, Advanced Skills Teachers, tutors from partnership Higher Education institutes; all observations should be co-ordinated by the tutor/mentor.

OBSERVATIONS OF EXPERIENCED TEACHERS

- The NQT should be given opportunities to observe experienced teachers in order to help to develop good practice in specific areas of teaching; this could be in the NQT's own school or in another where effective practice has been identified and could be particularly effective where the NQT is the sole teacher of a subject or aspect in a school;
- The focus of the observation should be based on the NQT's objectives for development and should relate to the requirements for satisfactory completion of induction.

OTHER INFORMATION AND ADVICE
Effective induction policies will help NQTs (and all other staff new to the school) to realise their full potential. They should expect to receive information and advice on the following:

- timetabling of lessons and support arrangements, names and contacts of induction tutors and a schedule for formal assessment and meetings;
- reporting arrangements and entitlements to pay during sickness absences, contacts for other absences, e.g. maternity leave;
- arrangements for salary payments, provision for pensions and any other entitlements;
- health and safety and equal opportunities policies;
- other relevant policies including arrangements for cover, child protection, etc.;
- the nature of the contract of employment, list of duties and management arrangements.

In most schools information and support already goes beyond this and there is great benefit to any new member of staff if free and open discussion takes place to identify the needs of new staff.

DfEE Circular 5/99 identifies a shared responsibility for the process and procedures of induction between the NQT, the tutor/mentor, the headteacher, the governing body and the appropriate body (the LEA for maintained schools).

The NQT should:

- make the Career Entry Profile available to the headteacher and tutor/mentor and should use this as a basis for setting short-, medium- and longer-term objectives for professional development;
- be familiar with the Induction Standards and should monitor his/her own work in relation to them;
- take increasing responsibility for his/her professional development as the induction period progresses.

The induction tutor/mentor should:

- be the NQT's line manager and may be the head, a senior member of staff or a suitably experienced teacher who has considerable contact with the NQT;
- be fully aware of the requirements of the induction period;
- have the necessary skills, expertise and knowledge to work effectively in the role;
- be able to make rigorous and fair judgements about the NQT's performance in relation to the requirements for satisfactory completion of the induction period;
- provide or co-ordinate guidance and effective support for the NQT's professional development;
- ensure that records are kept of the monitoring, support and formal assessment activities undertaken and their outcomes.

In addition to providing formative assessment, the tutor/mentor will, in many cases, be involved in the summative assessment at the end of the induction period. However, the support and assessment functions may be shared by two or more teachers where this suits the structure and systems of the school. In such circumstances, responsibilities should be clearly defined.

The headteacher:

- will be responsible, with the appropriate body, for the supervision and training of NQTs during their induction period;
- must recommend to the appropriate body whether the NQT has met the requirements for satisfactory completion of the induction period;

- must keep the governing body informed about the arrangements for the induction process and the results of any formal assessment meetings;
- should inform the appropriate body if any NQT, who has not yet completed an induction period, either joins or leaves the school;
- must ensure that records and reports are maintained, are received from schools where the NQT has part completed the induction period, and similarly are sent on to the NQT's new school where an NQT leaves before completing the induction period;
- must retain copies of all reports of observations, review meetings and objectives for the remainder of a five-year period.

The governing body should:

- when appointing new staff, take into account the school's responsibility to provide the necessary monitoring, support and assessment for NQTs.

The appropriate body:

- decides whether an NQT has met the Induction Standards based on the recommendations of the headteacher;
- has overall responsibility for the training and supervision during the induction period;
- will be required to inform the Secretary of State, the headteacher and the NQT of the outcome of induction, both for successful teachers and for those who fail induction or have their period of induction extended;
- when requested provides guidance, support and assistance to schools and training for teachers on their role of providing induction support, supervision and assessment.

Students on Teaching Practice (Trainees)

The same general principles applying to NQTs should be used for teachers on teaching practice although responsibilities are shared with the Higher Education institutions, particularly for those schools involved in the Initial Teacher Education Partnership.

Induction of other staff

The policies on induction of the school and of the team/department should also include reference to new appointments of experienced, part-time and supply teachers and support staff.

Experienced full-time and part-time teachers, and most temporary teachers, are likely to need the same information as NQTs but the level of support should not be as demanding. However, it is important that close contact is maintained with all new staff to ensure an effective settling-in period, particularly with reference to school and team/department routine procedures. Part-time teachers have the difficulty of continuity through the week and it is important that they are kept well informed of issues arising when they are not in school. Part-time teachers may also need additional help for collection of homework and access to teaching and learning resources.

Supply teachers may require less detailed information, perhaps in the form of abbreviated handbooks or a separate abridged document containing the essential elements with which they will be involved. They particularly need guidance on what they should do, or who they should contact, in case of any problems or difficulties.

Support staff involved with in-class support will need more information and guidance in relation to the curricular issues. Administrative and clerical staff will have their own needs in relation to whole school routines whereas departmental technical staff and other support staff should be regarded as members of the team without, of course, the same need for detail of the teaching programmes.

Although good induction systems are costly in terms of time and effort, the benefits gained should fully justify this. All members of the school community (including the pupils) work best when they feel valued and supported and this is particularly true of those new to the school. The culture of the school and the team is most important. The regular smile and enquiry about progress, and time rendered when necessary, will give the newcomers an immediate feeling that they are a part of the school/team.

Motivation of Staff

Successful teams are those whose members all have a high level of commitment, which arises from the motivation that the team members receive. They are all likely to be motivated when:

- there is a feeling of security and community in the team;
- there is confidence, and they are confident, in their abilities;
- there is a recognition of their:

  - worth;
  - competence;
  - special abilities;
  - contributions;

- they are empowered to contribute and are not simply given delegated tasks;
- they are, and feel, involved in formulation of policies, plans, etc.;
- there is a recognition of the time and effort they put in;
- there is a sense of improvement in the work of the team;
- expected outcomes are clear;
- success is celebrated;
- there is regular interchange of ideas, experiences and information;
- support and help are readily available if, and when, problems or difficulties arise;
- there is confidence in the leader, based on credibility and reputation for success;
- they enjoy their work, particularly with the team.

All of the above can increase motivation and develop self-motivation in staff, providing that they are applied in a regular, consistent and genuine way.

Teachers are least likely to be motivated when:

- they are told what to do;
- they are put in threatening or compromising positions;
- team planning is poor;
- much time and effort is put in without any obvious improvement or recognition;
- there is a lack of organisation and planning;
- mistakes, errors and omissions are criticised, while success is ignored.

A leader can take the following practical steps to increase motivation and commitment:

- increase the level of consultation and discussion, particularly at times of change;
- develop staff, especially their knowledge, understanding and skills, and thereby their confidence;
- make as much time as possible available for them;
- lead by example;
- involve all staff, teaching and support staff, where they think it relevant and appropriate;
- use all expertise available;
- encourage staff to 'air, share and compare' their views and opinions in an open and professional way;
- recognise success and build on it;
- recognise and appreciate the work done;
- empower staff, i.e. delegate authority and responsibility as well as the tasks to be undertaken.

Under-Performance of Teachers *(Supplement S5)*

The under-performance of teachers and a decline in the quality of their teaching is initially a team/departmental problem and responsibility, and to a large extent the responsibility of the team leader. The key elements in this are the effects on the quality of learning and the under-performance of the pupils in terms of their achievement and most likely their attitude and behaviour. This is likely to reflect on the team as a whole and, if the department is to act as a team, all members of the team have a part to play in helping to overcome the difficulties.

The following are possible causes of under-performance by teachers:

- a lack of the necessary skills and/or the ability to develop them;
- their existing work-load is beyond their capability;
- the timetabling has created groups with which they are unable to cope;
- they are 'difficult' people with perhaps some history of poor interpersonal relationships;
- they are not self-motivated and may need a great deal of help, support or supervision;
- they are not 'team players' in areas where team work is essential;
- self-interest always seems to be their main driving force;
- they are not flexible and do not adapt easily to change;
- they are 'dishonest' and do not adopt the positive approach of the rest of the team.

The problem can be attacked at 'team' level through help, support and guidance and perhaps further training. In most instances, good teamwork can solve many problems if they are tackled at an early enough stage but, failing that, action may need to pass to senior managers for more formal action.

Although support staff are not employed under the same terms and conditions of service as teachers, the same principles of tackling under-performance should be applied.

3 PUPIL MANAGEMENT

Promoting Good Behaviour *(Supplement TL2)*

In many school and team documents on pupil management, the policy often has the heading 'Discipline', which in itself implies problems and the means of dealing with poor attitudes, disruption or misbehaviour.

It is always preferable to look at the converse of this, by means of positive attempts to develop self-discipline through motivating pupils and developing their self-esteem. Pupils have positive attitudes and characteristics when they feel that:

- they are valued by the teachers and other staff;
- teachers are approachable through informal as well as formal relationships;
- they have opportunities to display their talents and enthusiasms;
- they are treated as responsible 'adults';
- they are valued by their friends and peers;
- they are able to talk through their problems with sympathetic adults;
- good and poor behaviour are dealt with in a consistent way;
- rewards and sanctions are applied in a reasonable, 'fair' way.

The school will certainly have statements within the aims which emphasise some of these issues and it is important that team documentation makes comment on the positive aspects of pupil/pupil and pupil/staff relationships. In deciding on rewards and sanctions it is important to stress the consistency in these relationships. Rewards are important but must be valued by the pupils and not awarded for trivial reasons as the rewards then lose their value in the eyes of the pupils. Similarly, use of sanctions should distinguish between the rebellious behaviour that might be a nuisance, is difficult to handle and is affecting the learning of those rebelling as well as others in the group; and rebellion that reflects a lively spirit or a more mature personality or a reasonable challenging of 'authority'. In some pupils an active, reflective, and thoughtful mind makes behavioural conformity difficult at times, even for those who are normally prepared to show commitment and co-operation.

Whilst the vast majority of interpersonal relationships in schools are positive, there will be instances where these relationships break down and the behaviour of individual pupils or groups becomes unacceptable. Because of the number of people involved, schools always have a problem of dealing with misbehaviour in a uniform and consistent way but, at a team level, with fewer teachers involved, consistency ought to be easier to achieve. Teams/departments should accept responsibility for the application of a rewards/sanctions system, in line with any school policies, and should work in liaison with pastoral/tutorial staff or members of the school management team as appropriate.

Special Educational Needs

There is a common assumption that special educational need applies only to those pupils who, at some time in their educational career, have a greater difficulty in learning, in particular subject areas, than their peers. However, because pupils learn at different rates and in different ways (both of which may vary over time) it is important that the learning for all pupils is sufficiently differentiated to provide challenging, but realistic targets, including targets for the most able (see Differentiation, pp. 52–4).

Whenever pupils enter the school, data on prior achievement (no matter what levels have been achieved) and other information relating to possible effects on learning form an essential part of the process of development of differentiation of teaching and learning.

Pupils with Statements of Special Educational Need will have an Individual Education Plan (IEP). This is drawn up by the school in consultation with the external Support Services and the parents of the pupils. Teams or individual teachers may well identify the need initially and may be involved in the process of drawing up the statement and the IEP. Because of the different problems that may arise in different subject areas, it may also be the responsibility of the team to monitor the progress of the pupil and to give feedback on the implementation of the IEP. The team may also be required to provide evidence of the pupil's progress for the Annual Review procedure.

Particular difficulties may arise in some subject areas where the special needs relate to visual, aural, oral and physical impairment, emotional and behavioural difficulties or any combination of these. This may have health and safety implications for the SEN pupil as well as the other pupils in the group. However, the school is statutorily bound to ensure that the National Curriculum is provided for all pupils of compulsory school age as an entitlement, and there is a clear expectation that departures from the norm will be few. Where there are such departures from the National Curriculum requirements, departments must be aware of the precise details of modification or disapplication that will be identified in the pupil's Statement of Special Educational Need.

The team should liaise closely with the school's Head of Special Needs, or the SENCO, to ensure that all policies and practices of the team meet the Code of Practice and the school's Special Educational Needs policies.

In schools where a separate team for SEN exists, the detailed documentation relating to the whole process within the Code of Practice must form a part of the SEN team's documentation. There is also a need to ensure that each of the other teams has access to information and the required procedures, generally through a 'nominated' person in each team.

A document entitled *National Standards for Special Educational Needs Co-ordinators* was produced at the same time as the *National Standards for Subject Leaders* (TTA 1998). While it is an essential document for the middle management role of SENCOs, all middle managers would gain by referring to it. The document contains all the essential elements of special needs, many of which have direct implications for all other middle and senior managers in schools.

Differentiation *(Supplements TL2–TL5)*

OFSTED has defined differentiation simply as:

> the process through which pupils of all abilities can show what they know, understand and can do.

It involves:

- enabling every pupil to get started – pupils must be able to understand the initial task, which must be appropriate, and language used should reflect the varying levels of ability of the pupils;

- enabling all pupils to make some progress irrespective of their ability;
- setting related but different tasks, or common tasks that can be completed successfully at different levels;
- constructing a scheme of work with a clearly identifiable common core in which the essentials of each session/topic must be covered by the least able in the group;
- providing a range or variety of approaches that will enable pupils, other than the least able, to be extended; in addition there should be extra or different approaches to the work which will challenge the most able.

Differentiation of teaching and learning forms a most essential part of the development of schemes of work and the translation of these into lesson plans. While the existence of the need for differentiation is obvious, implementation of successful schemes, to encompass the broad range of learning ability, is difficult.

The pupils' learning characteristics, which necessitate differentiation, include:

- age/maturity;
- intellectual ability;
- health;
- physical ability;
- personality;
- motivation;
- level and length of concentration;
- previous learning experiences;
- learning styles.

The last of these is the aspect which is most frequently omitted when planning lessons. Kolb's (1984) work on learning styles (*Supplement TL3*) indicates a range of learning types and the categorisation is meant to indicate the range which might exist in any group of learners. The learning experiences have, therefore, to take into account the needs of the learners; teaching in one style only will not allow for the differentiation needed. Some teachers teach in a way that perhaps matches their own learning styles. As all teachers have been successful learners, this approach may be more likely to suit only the successful (able) pupils in their teaching groups.

The use of the exercise in *Supplement TL3*, as a team or school in-service activity, can yield quite surprising results about the teaching and learning processes and the teachers' perceptions of them. It can provide a good start to the consideration of differentiation which is so often raised as a weakness in the work of some teams. If the language in the exercise were modified, it could also be used, within a tutorial or subject lesson, with groups of pupils to identify the range of learner types within the groups. This would, for many teachers and perhaps the pupils, produce some quite revealing information about the learner needs in the groups and might also help the pupils to understand their strengths as learners and the areas in need of development. In addition this type of exercise might also help the pupils in their target setting.

Techniques which may help to overcome the problems of the wide variety of learning styles and abilities include:

- pupil grouping:

  - streaming or setting across the year group which may be a school policy decision;
  - setting within a subject which may be a decision for the department to make;

  - grouping within teaching groups;
  - varying teaching organisation to include individual, paired and group work;

- class/teaching group sizes;
- variety in the types and levels of tasks to be set for, and undertaken by, different pupils;
- variety in teaching methodologies to account for the range of learning styles;
- variety of teaching and learning resources to cater for the range of learner styles and reading ages;
- in-class support (non-teaching assistants, other support staff, 'senior' pupils, parents, other adults);
- classroom organisation and management;
- additional time;
- differentiation of the anticipated outcomes.

Self-assessment

The work of pupils in England is assessed more often than in many other European countries. However, the vast majority of this assessment is 'external', is summative and is rarely diagnostic. As with all learning, self-assessment, particularly as it is usually diagnostic, is a much more effective means of assessment and can also improve motivation. Most pupils, like many teachers, tend to underestimate their abilities and capabilities, usually because of a fear of being found wanting, or in some instances not wanting to appear as 'swots' or 'goodies' to their peers. However, positive, diagnostic self-assessment can be a powerful influence in increasing pupil achievement and motivation.

The National Record of Achievement has gone some way to involving pupils in their own assessment but some of the approaches used have led to pupils becoming disenchanted with the process because they have not been given sufficient training or variety in the assessments that they have been expected to make. In addition, there has often been insufficient follow-up by some teachers, which has lessened the value of these assessments in the eyes of the pupils.

Target Setting by Pupils

Target setting, by staff for pupils and by the pupils themselves, has now become a much more common feature in schools, although the process has existed for many years in effective schools. Target setting follows on naturally from pupil self-assessment, but again the pupils need practice in this process. What should be aimed for is a process of encouragement for the pupils to develop their own Individual Educational Plans (see p. 52), but without the need for the statutory requirements. Pupils in Years 10 and 11 and in sixth forms do tend to set some broad-ranging targets in relation to external examinations, but practice in this area should begin much earlier if pupils are to become proficient in setting challenging but realistic targets.

Since pupils tend to underestimate their abilities they will usually set themselves targets well within their reach, although there are, of course, exceptions to this. They may fear or worry about not reaching their targets, i.e. build in a failure element; for some pupils, setting undemanding targets makes for an easier life. Pupils need training in the setting of demanding, but realistic targets for their learning and development.

This training should occur in each subject but there are many instances where work of this kind can be (if not already) introduced in more general ways in tutor periods or whole class time.

Target setting is one area in which subject teams need to maintain a close liaison with pastoral staff. In more effective schools, the pastoral/academic divide does not exist as there is an understanding of the complementary roles of the staff concerned. Pastoral staff have responsibilities that extend beyond the 'Good Shepherd' philosophy to an overview of the pupils' personal, social and academic development. Problems arise when there is too much concern with the roles, responsibilities and status of the middle managers involved. If there is professional acceptance of the differing, but complementary, roles of all teachers for all aspects of pupils' development, without fear of 'treading on the professional toes' of other staff, the pupils will inevitably benefit.

Documentation, therefore, needs to be clear in the approach that all members of the department should take in their liaison work with 'pastoral' staff, all of whom are likely to be members of subject teams.

Negligence

The duty of all teachers to secure the physical safety of pupils arises in a number of ways, as follows.

- The condition of school premises:

  - Premises must not endanger pupils, staff or visitors to the school;
  - The school must be properly equipped to deal with safety aspects, e.g. fire escape procedures and fire-fighting equipment;
  - Routine maintenance should cover such matters as the physical state of the teaching areas and of gas, water and electrical services;

- Safety in the teaching areas and playing fields:

  - All lessons must be conducted in a safe manner, particularly those with inherent dangers, e.g. PE and games, science and technology. Risks have to be assessed and guarded against as a part of the health and safety policies of the school and the team. PE and games equipment, laboratory apparatus and all electrical, mechanical and fire-fighting equipment must be checked regularly and, where appropriate, tagged and marked with the date of inspection. Fire-fighting equipment will probably be checked by the Fire Brigade and any doubts about any other items should be referred to a specialist adviser, normally through the LEA;
  - There is a particular obligation to ensure that those in charge of potentially dangerous activities are suitably qualified and trained. This is an increased duty on teachers because of the vulnerability of children;
  - All aspects of health and safety (see p. 69) are also relevant, e.g. when pupils are out-of-doors for long periods in extremes of weather conditions;

- First aid and other medical issues:

  - First-aid materials and equipment should be available around the school, but they must be readily and easily accessible in areas of greater risk, e.g. PE areas, science laboratories, food technology areas and the workshops. Schools should also have at least one first-aider available at all times and it is an obvious advantage if there is someone with at least basic first-aid experience in each team;

- Where any doubt exists about the seriousness of an injury, medical expertise should always be sought. Where injured pupils need off-site medical attention, they should be accompanied, preferably by their parents, but medical personnel have a legal duty to accept responsibility where no other adult is available;
- The school will have a system for recording all instances of injury to pupils but it is important for the staff concerned, as soon as possible after an incident, to make a note of it and of any initial treatment given;

• Supervision:

- Most schools have rules concerning pupils in school and the supervision arrangements. Clearly, certain areas are potentially more dangerous and pupils should not be allowed to enter without supervision. The school must make a risk assessment;
- Potential dangers can also exist where areas, even general classrooms, are used for pre-school, lunchtime and after-school clubs and activities;
- The same principles, regarding the duties of teachers, apply to other out-of-school activities such as field trips and outdoor pursuits, some of which present potentially dangerous situations. Because of recent tragic incidents, most LEAs have issued clear guidance on these activities, based on DfEE recommendations (see p. 205), and teachers should follow these at all times. For departments carrying out field work or involved in outdoor pursuits there are often stringent safety regulations which must be followed. In most of these instances, additional insurance should always be considered (see pp. 69–70).

4 RESOURCE MANAGEMENT

Although the main resource in any team/department is the teaching and support staff, this section is concerned mainly with the resources for learning and teaching.

Traditionally, the selection and ordering of learning and teaching resources was one of the main responsibilities of the heads of teams, if not their sole responsibility outside their own teaching programmes. It remains an important issue, largely because of financial constraints and the increase in the costs of many items in recent years, but it should have a less critical role compared with the leadership and management of other, more important areas.

Schemes of work should contain references to the learning and teaching resources available with suggestions as to how these might best be used. In order to make optimum use of the resources the team should monitor and review the resource provision including those resources external to the school, which may be environmental and/or human.

Learning and teaching resources may be listed and catalogued under the following headings, with the locations of each identified, where appropriate, in the scheme of work:

- appropriate text books;
- appropriate workbooks/worksheets – purchased and self-produced;
- reference materials – class, subject and school library items;
- ICT provision (hardware and software) – subject and school items;
- collections and display materials;
- audio-visual materials;
- materials, tools and equipment.

In addition, there are resources which are external to the school:

- LEA support and loan services;
- local resources – sports centres, swimming pools, libraries, art galleries, theatres, etc.;
- other establishments – schools, colleges of F.E. and H.E. institutions;
- local industrial and commercial organisations;
- field study and outdoor pursuits centres;
- locations, sites and centres for environmental science/study, history, etc.;
- centres for physical education, sport and leisure activities.

The use of many of the resources, particularly those outside the school, requires consideration of health and safety issues which should be included alongside the resource. There will be requirements to follow school and LEA policies for some of these, particularly those outside school hours and those with potential danger, which may need additional staffing, insurance, etc. Where any uncertainty exists, advice should be sought before entering into any arrangements. LEAs are likely to have more detailed information or will be able to investigate on behalf of the school. In addition, guidance on these aspects of health and safety is contained in a booklet, *Health and Safety of Pupils on Educational Visits* (DfEE 1998).

In addition to classifying and cataloguing resources, there must be a routine for evaluating the resources used, particularly before a commitment is made to purchase or where new materials are being used for the first time.

There should be a routine for maintaining a record of materials in order that losses and breakages can be identified. The school and/or the LEA may have policies for the maintenance of an official departmental/team inventory of all equipment and materials, usually those items costing above a certain value (normally the purchase price), e.g. £50 or £100. These inventories are subject to external audit.

5 INFORMATION AND COMMUNICATIONS TECHNOLOGY (ICT) IN TEACHING, ORGANISATION, MANAGEMENT AND ADMINISTRATION

Reference is made throughout this book to the use of information technology as a means of storing and retrieving data in order to improve the quality of teaching and learning, organisation, management and administration. Most schools and LEAs now make extensive use of information and communications technology, largely for management and administrative purposes, through some form of management information system. However, a key part of the government's strategy for education is to provide teachers with the opportunity to exploit further the potential of ICT to raise pupils' standards of achievement.

This is being financed through the New Opportunities Fund (NOF) and supported by the National Grid for Learning (NGfL) which as a resource is intended to improve the quality and availability of educational materials and to increase and widen access to learning for all. It also includes resources to support the professional development of teachers.

Targets

The government has set out the following targets for the development of the NGfL:

- by 1999:

  - all newly qualified teachers should be ICT literate;

- by 2002:

  - serving teachers should generally feel confident, and competent to teach, using ICT within the curriculum;
  - all schools, colleges, universities and libraries should be connected to the Grid;
  - most school leavers should have a good understanding of ICT;
  - the UK should be a centre for excellence in the development of networked software;
  - general administrative communications to schools should be electronic, not paper-based.

The NGfL is a completely free service and first time users simply register their interests. On subsequent visits to the website all that is needed is to log on and use the information in the pamphlet produced by the DfEE and the British Educational Communications and Technology agency (BECTa), copies of which should be in all schools.

The TTA has produced a pamphlet, *The Use of ICT in Subject Teaching: Expected Outcomes for Teachers (England, Wales and Northern Ireland)*, and a series of additional pamphlets to allow schools and teachers to begin to identify future training needs for the use of ICT. These pamphlets cover the following subjects and areas:

- for teachers of pupils up to the age of 11 in English, mathematics and science, the other compulsory subjects of the Northern Ireland Curriculum and, where relevant, Welsh;

- for teachers of pupils aged 11 and above in English, mathematics, science, history, geography, modern foreign languages, design and technology, information technology, music, art, physical education, religious education, business studies, Irish and Welsh;
- more general pamphlets for primary teachers, senior managers, and for group training needs.

Copies of all of these pamphlets should be in all schools. It is strongly recommended that all middle managers should have, in addition to those that they need for the subject(s) they teach, their own copies of the general pamphlets on:

- the overview for senior managers;
- group training needs;
- the use of ICT in subject teaching;
- the primary pamphlet.

Copies of any or all of these may be obtained by telephoning the TTA or they can be accessed from the TTA's website (see p. 200). A more extensive and interactive version of the needs identification materials is available on CD-ROM, which can be reviewed on the appropriate VTC website (see p. 200).

Expected Outcomes

The principal aim of the ICT training is based on Expected Outcomes and is intended to equip teachers with the necessary knowledge, skills and understanding to make decisions about when, when not, and how to use ICT effectively in teaching particular subjects in the relevant phase. Although the Expected Outcomes apply to all teachers, the level required will vary between specialism, subjects and phases. The training will be provided by nationally approved agencies to ensure that the training is firmly rooted within subject and phase, rather than being about how to use ICT generically or as an end itself.

The Expected Outcomes for teachers include:

- knowledge and understanding of the contribution that the different aspects of ICT can make to teaching particular subjects;
- effective planning, including the use of ICT for lesson preparation and the choice and organisation of ICT resources;
- the use of ICT in whole class teaching;
- assessment of pupils' learning of the subject when ICT has been used;
- the use of ICT to keep up to date, share best practice and reduce bureaucracy.

Many teachers and school librarians will already have the knowledge and skills set out in the Expected Outcomes and will therefore not need the training through the NOF initiative. This training is aimed only at those who need to develop their knowledge, skills and understanding up to the standard required in the Expected Outcomes (see examples, p. 61).

Training will cover a wide range of subjects for teachers in the secondary phase and will focus on English, mathematics and science in the primary phase, with particular emphasis on the effective use of ICT in teaching literacy and numeracy. The key features of the NOF training initiative in ICT for teachers include:

- the integration of training in the use of ICT in teaching the subject in the relevant phase;
- a majority of training to be school-based and to involve the use of ICT in the classroom;
- support for the development and use of the National Grid for Learning;
- training preceded by the identification and prioritisation of individual needs against the Expected Outcomes.

Examples of the Expected Outcomes

For those aspects of lessons where ICT is to be used, teachers should be able to identify in their planning:

- the way(s) in which ICT will be used to meet teaching and learning objectives in the subject;
- key questions to ask and opportunities for teacher intervention in order to stimulate and direct pupils' learning;
- the way(s) in which pupils' progress will be assessed and recorded;
- criteria to ensure that judgements about pupils' attainment and progress in the subject are not masked because ICT has been used;
- any impact of the use of ICT on the organisation and conduct of the subject lesson and how this is managed;
- how the ICT used is appropriate to the particular subject-related objectives in hand and to pupils' capabilities, taking into account the fact that some pupils may already be competent . . . and some may need additional support.

Teachers should be competent in those areas of ICT which support pedagogy in every subject, including that they:

- can employ common ICT tools for their own and pupils' benefit, *e.g. word processing, e-mail, presentation software, data handling*, and can use a range of ICT resources at the level of general users including:

  - the common uses of interfaces, using menus, selecting and swapping between applications, cutting, pasting and copying files, and cutting, copying and pasting data within and between applications;
  - successfully connecting and setting up ICT equipment, including input devices, *e.g. a mouse, touch screen, overlay keyboard, microphone*, and output devices, *e.g. printers, screens and loudspeakers*;
  - loading and running software, *e.g. a CD-ROM*;
  - file management, *e.g. organising documents and folders*;
  - seeking and using operating information, including from on-line help facilities and user guides;
  - coping with everyday problems and undertaking simple, routine maintenance, with due consideration to health and safety;
  - understanding the importance of passwords and the general security of equipment and access to it;

- know and understand the characteristics of information, including:

  - that information must be evaluated in terms of its accuracy, validity, reliability, plausibility and bias;

- that information has to be stored somewhere, it takes up memory (storage space) and that there are implications when saving and compressing files;
- that ICT systems can present static information or changing information;
- that information can be directly and dynamically linked between applications;
- that applications and information can be shared with other people at remote locations.

(*The Use of ICT in Subject Teaching*, TTA 1999)

6 FINANCIAL MANAGEMENT

Departmental, Subject and Team Finances

The maintenance of clear, accurate and up-to-date records of all of the department/ team finances, whatever the source of that finance, is most important. The school's management information system is likely to maintain the records of finance of each department or subject area but it is important that someone in the department/team takes responsibility for the monitoring of expenditure and income. It should not be necessary to replicate the records which are held centrally, providing these are readily accessible, but there is a need to maintain some form of record to avoid overspending or underspending towards the end of the financial year. The team should also carry out its own internal audit as well as the external audit of all finances that the school will face.

The departmental/team development plan will have identified priority elements for expenditure on planned initiatives and the anticipated levels of spending. These will need to be reviewed throughout the year to ensure that the team is gaining maximum value for money (see p. 64).

Acquisition of Resources (Procurement)

To ensure regularity and propriety in the handling of public funds (or indeed funds generated from any source), the general advice is:

- don't bend or break the rules;
- put in place and follow clear procedures;
- if approval is required, from the head, governors and/or the LEA, PTA or other body, get that approval first;
- don't allow a conflict of interests to affect, or appear to affect, decisions on spending;
- don't use 'public money' for private benefit;
- be even-handed;
- keep a record of reasons for purchasing decisions, e.g. choice from a number of estimates.

Whilst the amounts of money available for departmental/team disposal may be small, these guidelines should, nonetheless, be kept in mind.

Value for Money

Finance for schools and teams will always be somewhat restricted and it is important to ensure that the best value for money is achieved on all occasions.

Most LEAs will have contractual arrangements with suppliers which will generally provide both goods and services at lower prices. LEAs and ISIS may also have expertise in purchasing and in the legislation relating to the rights of the purchaser.

Value for money is not just about getting items or services at the lowest price, it also includes:

- fitness for purpose (e.g. quality of goods or services);
- delivery and availability against price;

- the 'cost' of ownership (e.g. any lease arrangements, maintenance and running costs);
- 'on costs' (for example, delivery and storage);
- the cost of purchase (e.g. the cost of the time spent on selecting and effecting the purchase);
- anticipated life span/depreciation of the items to be purchased.

It follows that the best value for money does not necessarily mean the cheapest. Value for money can be summarised in the following 'five rights':

- the right quality;
- of the right quantity;
- at the right price;
- to the right place;
- at the right time.

In assessing the suitability of resources, consideration should also be given to the 'three Es':

- Economy – minimising the cost of resources without sacrificing the appropriate quality, e.g. does the department seek several quotations?
- Efficiency – deploying just sufficient resources to achieve the desired results, e.g. is the time well spent?
- Effectiveness – achieving a close match between the actual results of a project and the intended results, e.g. has the purchase and introduction of new items, materials or schemes improved the quality of teaching, learning and the achievement of the pupils?

'Value for Money' (cost-effectiveness) could be expressed as the extent to which the departmental/team aims are achieved at minimum cost and is therefore a function of the 'three Es'.

Internal Controls

The school should have set procedures for the purchase of resources. However, as a budget holder, the team will usually decide on items to be purchased. The purchase orders are normally placed by a secretary or bursar, a copy of the order being retained. When goods arrive, they should be checked by someone independent of the team and, providing all is correct, the invoice should be returned to the secretary or bursar for payment. It is important that the ordering, checking and payment are done independently.

Where appropriate, newly purchased items should be entered in the team's inventory, recording serial numbers, supplier, date of purchase, etc. Any warranties or guarantees should be registered and filed. Valuable items should also be security marked with the school post code (e.g. by using an 'invisible marker pen').

Laws Relating to Sale and Supply of Goods and Services

There are three basic laws relating to the supply of goods and services (Sale of Goods Act 1979, Supply of Goods and Services Act 1982 and Unfair Contract Terms Act 1977). Where problems occur schools/teams should seek specialist advice, usually through the LEA, concerning the provisions of these laws and the duties that they impose on both the supplier and the purchaser. Any protracted attempt to resolve continuing difficulties with suppliers is likely to be frustrating and time-consuming and is usually done more effectively by LEAs who will have officers who are experienced in the procedures.

Accountability

Because schools are largely publicly funded, they have additional responsibilities beyond seeking value for money. They must be seen to achieve value for money, must deal fairly with suppliers and must have in place procurement systems which protect staff from allegations of prejudice or malpractice.

Charging Policy

The charging provisions of the Education Reform Act 1988 apply to all maintained schools, including nursery and special schools as well as Sixth Form Colleges. Although City Technology Colleges (CTCs) and City Colleges for the Technology of the Arts (CCTAs), like independent schools, are not covered by the Act there is a clear expectation that they will operate on the same basis.

The school, therefore, has a statutory responsibility to have a policy for charging and for the remission of charges. This will be a part of the school's documentation and it is most important to check it before writing a summary for guidance at team level. This guidance should include appropriate and relevant reference to the following.

Prohibited Charges

The underlying principle is that education should be free of charge if it takes place wholly or mainly within school hours, not counting the mid-day break. LEAs and governing bodies must have, and must implement, a charging policy and keep it under review. The policy must provide for charges for board and lodging to be remitted in full for all pupils whose parents are in receipt of income support or family credit, in the case of an activity that relates to the National Curriculum or takes place wholly or mainly within school hours. Other charges may be remitted partially or wholly in line with the policy.

There is a total prohibition of charging for:

- admission to a maintained school;
- the National Curriculum;
- anything that is required as a part of a syllabus for a prescribed public examination, such as GCSE, GNVQ and A level;
- examination entry fees, in the case of public examinations for which registered pupils are being prepared. Schools and LEAs can, however, recover examination fees where a pupil fails 'without good reason' to meet the relevant examination

requirements, e.g. incomplete coursework or unacceptable reason for absence from the examination or part of it. Where the school does not recommend entry for an examination, the parents have the right to pay for the entry and if the pupil should pass, the fee would normally be reimbursed to the parents;

- religious education;
- the provision of books, equipment (excluding clothing but including, for example, safety glasses), materials or transport in relation to any activity for which charges cannot be made. It is lawful, however, to charge for the supply of materials or ingredients where the parents have expressed a wish to keep the finished product. The cost of travelling to and from home when pupils are on work experience would normally be met by the parents, but not if travelling to another establishment for a prescribed course;
- non-residential school trips and visits that take place substantially (50 per cent or more) within school hours. A contribution to the costs may be requested, but it must be made clear to the parents that they are under no obligation to pay. No pupils may be excluded from such a trip because their parents have not contributed. If a particular trip is dependent on voluntary funding and insufficient funds are raised, the trip will have to be cancelled or the school must find the shortfall from its own resources. There is, however, nothing to prevent schools from notifying parents that such trips can go ahead only if sufficient income is generated.

Permissible Charges

Charging is permitted for:

- instrumental tuition (other than that required by the National Curriculum), individually or in groups of up to four. However, vocal/singing tuition, on an individual or group basis, must be free of charge;
- residential school trips (one or more nights away) in certain circumstances. The duration of the trip is divided into half-days which is 12 hours from midnight or noon, as the case may be. If at least 6 hours of a half-day are spent on a trip, that half-day counts as a part of the trip. If the number of school sessions missed is less than 50 per cent of the number of half-days spent on the trip, the trip is deemed to take place outside school hours and a charge can be made for the full trip. For example, a trip starting at noon on Wednesday and finishing at 10 pm on Sunday, i.e. 9 half-days, including 5 school sessions, would be regarded as taking place within school hours, but a trip starting at noon on Thursday and finishing at 10 pm on Sunday, i.e. 7 half-days, including 3 school sessions, would not. The board and lodging element of a residential trip may also be charged for, irrespective of whether the trip is deemed to have occurred within school hours or not, or whether the trip is undertaken to fulfil the requirements of the National Curriculum or religious education or a part of a prescribed examination board syllabus;
- non-residential school trips, visits and activities where the majority of time spent on the activity (including travelling time) is spent out of school hours. Thus a charge may be made for an evening theatre visit but a matinee performance is likely to fall mostly within school hours; all the school can do is ask for voluntary contributions. It must, however, be remembered that if an external examination syllabus specifies such visits, which is rare, no charge can be levied even if the visit takes place out of school hours;

- 'optional extras' (activities which by definition take place outside school hours or are advertised as optional). Participation in such activities is dependent on parental choice. A charge (including board and lodging where relevant) may be made, but it must not exceed the actual cost of the provision and should not include an element of subsidy for other pupils wishing to attend and whose parents are unwilling, or unable, to make a contribution to the event.

7 ROUTINE ADMINISTRATIVE PROCEDURES

Within the area of routine procedures teams should seek to make as much use as possible of the information and communications technology available. The intention should always be to save time, particularly in the storage and retrieval of administrative data as well as teaching materials, and to reduce the amount of detail that has to be transmitted, or permanently recorded, on paper.

Departmental/Team Records

Schools are advised, and may be required by LEA policy, to keep certain records relating to a range of issues which may have implications for future action (e.g. staff, pupil and financial records). Departments/teams are not required to keep such records and there is no point in duplicating any records held centrally in the school. However, consideration should be given to the following categories and it is worth making sure that the records are kept somewhere in the school and that they are readily accessible.

Pupil Details

Whilst the school will retain most records, departments/teams should consider keeping further details on pupils, in the form of the previous report made as well as continuous assessment information. This may be required if references on the pupil are requested or, although it is less likely, if the school has to face a later accusation of negligence in its educational provision. The school is required to keep examination results and curriculum development papers for six years and aggregated assessment results for five years. However, requests from former pupils are often made after a longer period has elapsed.

Financial Records

Where teams/departments are involved in any financial transactions, from school funds or from other sources, a record of these should be maintained. The recommended period for the retention of such records is six years. However, this may be shortened with the appropriate auditor's consent.

Equipment Records

The department/team must keep an inventory of all equipment. The LEA will normally have a base line figure of the value for items that need to be recorded. This, however, does not usually apply to disposable items even where these are bought in bulk and the value therefore exceeds the LEA baseline value. The inventory is subject to LEA audit and once an item is recorded it should only be deleted through the school or LEA official procedures. Some LEAs require notice of such deletions, particularly where unwanted items might be of use to another school. Records of equipment purchases, including receipts, warranties and guarantees, should be kept by the team/department, unless there is a central system for such records.

Health and Safety Records

These are normally kept centrally, particularly instances of accidents involving staff, pupils or visitors. However, a check should be made that there is no requirement for departments to keep their own or additional records.

OFSTED Inspection Records

The school will keep records of inspections (normally for six years), but it is valuable for teams/departments to keep their more detailed records, e.g. comments by inspectors and the feedback at the end of the inspection which may not have been recorded in the final report.

Health and Safety

The school must have a health and safety policy, which identifies and assesses the health and safety risks inherent in running the school. It must define responsibilities, show how the policy will be implemented and state how the implementation will be monitored.

All schools face similar issues on health and safety. These are issues that face all employers, except that there is an additional duty for health and safety in schools because of the age of the pupils involved. The governors have a duty to provide a safe workplace for staff, pupils and visitors, covering all aspects of the premises and their use, not merely the physical condition of the buildings. There are specific regulations for many areas of activity, for example:

*   control of hazardous materials, which is particularly important in science and technology departments as well as in some of the work of the caretaker and cleaning staff;
*   extended use of computer screens, which largely affects administrative staff;
*   food preparation – food technology departments and school kitchens;
*   handling of equipment;
*   electrical installations and equipment;
*   fire prevention and fighting equipment.

Although the headteacher is normally the person with overall responsibility for health and safety within the school, sometimes there is a member of staff designated as the 'premises controller' or health and safety representative. There is normally an internal health and safety committee with representation of the teachers' professional associations. However, staff have their own accountability. They are required to carry out their duties so as not to put themselves or others at risk and there is also a duty to co-operate with those responsible for health and safety, to implement health and safety measures and to report defects.

Insurance

Schools usually carry adequate insurance for premises and third party liability for staff, pupils and visitors. This is often a collective arrangement for LEA-maintained schools. However, this may not cover loss or theft of equipment, so some schools, having identified the level of cover, have invested in increased insurance. In addition, where risks to children and third parties are increased (e.g. for out-of-school activities and trips abroad), a greater level of insurance is advisable and professional advice should be sought if there is any uncertainty.

There is also a need for staff to check the insurance issues relating to carriage and use of school equipment off-site. In many instances, this may not be covered under the terms of the school's insurance policy and cover may rely on the teacher's own personal insurance policies. Similarly, there is a need to take care that there is insurance where teachers use their own cars to transport pupils and/or equipment and materials for both official or unofficial purposes.

Class/Subject/Departmental/Year Group and School Libraries

Many class teachers and teams retain copies of regularly used library and text books and other items. These should be listed and where there is a loan system for pupils the procedures for borrowing books and other materials should be identified.

School libraries have, in recent times, expanded rapidly into multi-media resource areas, many now providing interactive video and access to the Internet. It is important, in addition to any central documentation and advice, to have a guide to those items which are specific to the team/subject.

These may well be included in the section on teaching and learning resources where the centrally held resources provide better learning and teaching activities and opportunities.

Calendar

There should be a team/subject calendar which has all dates of school activities affecting the team, together with dates specific to the work of the team. As this calendar may be subject to changes during the year, it is better that it is displayed as a year planner at a strategic point where all members of the team have easy access.

Timetables

The team's documentation should also include the teaching timetables for staff and details of the groups that they teach, plus accommodation issues/constraints, particularly where teaching occurs outside specialist areas.

Rather than being in a handbook this is better displayed permanently and prominently.

Meetings

There are extremes of views on the value of team meetings. These range from a complete reliance on informal contact with colleagues, before and after school or during school breaks, to formal meetings to solve all problems. Neither of these extremes is adequate to cover the planning, review and evaluation of the department's work. The value of the day-to-day informal contacts should not be lost but these should be supplemented by scheduled, well-organised, formal meetings for planning, monitoring, review and evaluation.

Much valuable time is lost through poorly organised meetings which often fail to meet their intended outcomes. Meetings should be identified and programmed, as far as possible, across the full academic year. Some of these meetings may have prescribed agenda items because of the time of the year (e.g. regarding internal examinations or tests, public examination entries).

For those working singly or in small teams it is important to make use of other colleagues rather than trying to 'go it alone'. Colleagues from related subjects or members of the school management team should be used to help in the process.

In order to get the best from meetings, the following points should be considered:

- Before the meeting:
  - decide on the purpose of the meeting and ensure that all staff are aware of this purpose;
  - set clear objectives for the meeting and the start and finish times, and adhere strictly to these;
  - generate an agenda, consulting others for views on items to be included;
  - circulate the agenda and any relevant papers in advance of the meeting;
  - decide who will be Chair and who will take minutes; it is often better to share these responsibilities and it may be that a member of the school management team will take one of these roles; however, the team leader has overall responsibility and should be confident that the meeting and agenda are relevant and necessary.

- During the meeting:
  - the Chair should briefly review the agenda and the objectives, although it may be that one member with a specific responsibility should outline the relevant issue;
  - there should be an attempt to seek views from all members rather than having the meeting dominated by the most vocal;
  - periodically review progress to avoid the problem of going round and round the same issue;
  - attempt to arrive at a consensus but always avoid the temptation to have a vote (voting means that there are winners and losers); where consensus is not reached, it may be necessary for the team leader to take responsibility for the decision; however, when a critical or controversial issue remains undecided, it may be necessary to defer the item to a later meeting;
  - at the end of the meeting, the Chair should summarise the outcomes of the meeting, the decisions made and any action to be taken by members of the team.

- After the meeting:
  - check that the minutes are compiled, checked and circulated;
  - check that the minutes contain the decisions made, on the set objectives, and that those responsible for taking action are aware of what they have to do and the timescale for completion;
  - where there has been an unresolved item, because of lack of consensus, seek views from individuals in order to prepare for the next time that this is discussed;
  - seek views and feelings of all the staff about the meeting and how the process might be improved.

School Administrative Procedures

Where there is a staff handbook for the school, most of these procedures will be covered. However, it is worth checking that any issues not covered, or any variations or extensions from the school routines, are included in the team's documentation (e.g. issue of books and stationery, photocopying). This is particularly valuable to part-time, 'temporary', and supply teachers as well as teachers in training, who may not have ready access to the staff handbook.

Correspondence Procedures and Reports *(Supplement M3)*

Most schools will have policies or guidelines relating to procedures and a house style for correspondence, both in-coming and out-going, and this should be recorded within the team's documentation (e.g. all letters typed, on school-headed paper and over the head's signature). Where departments have a delegated responsibility for sending and receiving correspondence, guidance should be given on the procedures to be adopted, such as whether school-headed paper is required and whether letters are checked before being sent out. The latter point is important as one of the most common criticisms of letters from schools, particularly those to parents, is that they have errors of spelling, punctuation or grammar!

Most teachers rarely have to write long reports. Much of a teacher's writing is for personal use and is, therefore, often abbreviated or written in note form, as time rarely allows for much more. Increasingly, however, departments have to produce reports for external consumption, and guidance on this is given in *Supplement M3*.

Centrally Held Resources

The team's documentation should also include a list of the school's centrally held resources and the procedures for obtaining or booking these. Such resources may include specialist rooms (e.g. ICT rooms, rooms set up for larger groups or for TV viewing). Lists of centrally held audio visual aids should also be recorded and, since these are subject to change as newer or more effective aids are acquired by the school, they should be updated periodically.

Part 2

Part 2

Key Elements of the Role of Middle Managers

LEADERSHIP

A leader:

- understands the aims of the school, and how the work of the team may support these aims;
- understands that all people are different from each other and tries to create interest, challenge and enjoyment in work for everybody;
- optimises the professional expertise, skills and abilities of all members of the team to improve – improvement and innovation are the aims;
- is an unceasing learner, encouraging the team to study and providing opportunities for professional development;
- is a coach and counsellor, not a judge;
- understands a stable system – how to make use of people's abilities, aptitudes and strengths, and how to identify their weaknesses and failures and help them to overcome these;
- has three sources of power – formal position, knowledge and personality; a successful leader develops the second and third of these and does not rely on the first, but does use it when appropriate as this enables change to the system in order to bring improvement;
- investigates and evaluates learning outcomes and other results with the aim of improving performance;
- identifies members of the team who are outside the system and provides them with special help;
- creates trust, freedom and innovation but also realises that the creation of trust requires the taking of risks;
- does not expect perfection (the vision) but strives for it;
- listens and learns without passing judgement on those who are speaking;
- understands the benefits of co-operation and the losses resulting from competition between people and groups.

(Adapted from Neave 1990)

LEADERSHIP, MANAGEMENT AND ADMINISTRATION

Throughout a career in teaching everyone operates, to different extents and at different times, within the roles of leader, manager and administrator. The extent to which one operates in each of these roles is dependent on a number of interrelated factors, such as position of responsibility, expectations of others, confidence and competence, enthusiasm, initiative, vision, involvement, commitment, the management structure and the existing culture of the school and the department/subject/team, etc. The lists in Table 2 give somewhat 'tongue in cheek' and polarised, but nonetheless appropriate, descriptions of the three roles.

Table 2 Characteristics of the leader, manager and administrator

The Leader	*The Manager*	*The Administrator*
Devises and develops	Advises and plans	Maintains
Innovates	Organises	Does the paperwork
Challenges the status quo	Works with the status quo	Operates the status quo
Takes the longer-term view	Takes a shorter-term view	Works to the shortest-term view
Asks why, what and who?	Asks when, how and how much?	Is told when, how and how much
Looks to the horizon	Looks at the bottom line	Works to the bottom line
Focuses on people	Focuses on systems	Operates the system
Inspires trust and confidence	Relies on control	Complies with the controls
Does the right thing	Does things right	Ensures things are done in the time and cost set

Source: Adapted from Bennis (1969).

In addition to a teaching commitment, middle managers have to operate in all three roles, dependent on the task in hand, but there is an increasing need to operate at the 'leadership' end of the continuum. It is through continued professional development that the abilities to operate 'more to the left' are improved.

There are also key questions which need to be considered at school, subject/department or year group level in the process of reviewing the roles of all leaders in schools:

- How are the roles of leader, manager and administrator currently distributed in the school:

  - within the governing body?
  - in the school management team?
  - among the middle managers?

  – within your department/team or year groups?
  – within other departments/teams or year groups?
  – among the other staff (teaching and non-teaching)?
  – among the pupils?

• What is the rationale for these distributions?
• Is this the best organisation in terms of managing change effectively and improving the quality of the work of the departments or teams?
• Are there better alternatives; if so, what, and who should take the necessary action to implement the changes?
• What action needs to be taken to ensure that every member of staff (teaching and support staff) has opportunities to be both a leader and a manager in relevant areas and at appropriate times?
• Is this to be done by simply delegating tasks or through empowerment of responsibility – can the present culture of the school/team cope with this?
• How might this improve the quality of learning and teaching and thereby the standards of achievement by the pupils?

NATIONAL STANDARDS FOR SUBJECT LEADERS

In 1998, the Teacher Training Agency produced a series of four documents on National Standards in the following areas:

- The award of Qualified Teacher Status (QTS);
- Special Educational Needs Co-ordinators (SENCOs);
- Subject Leaders;
- Headteachers.

The main aims of these National Standards are to:

- set out clear expectations for teachers at key points in the profession;
- help teachers at different points in the profession to plan and monitor their development, training and performance effectively, and to set clear, relevant targets for improving their effectiveness;
- ensure that the focus at every point is on improving the achievement of pupils and the quality of their education;
- provide a basis for the professional recognition of teachers' expertise and achievements;
- help providers of professional development to plan and provide high quality, relevant training which meets the needs of individual teachers and headteachers, makes good use of their time and has the maximum benefit for the pupils.

The National Standards set out the professional knowledge, understanding, skills and attributes necessary to carry out effectively the key tasks in each of the four roles. It is the sum of these aspects which defines the expertise demanded of the role, in order to achieve the outcomes set out in each of the documents.

The standards emphasise national priorities, particularly in support of the present government's key educational targets in relation to literacy and numeracy as well as information and communications technology. The standards are intended to aid development rather than being barriers to progression in the profession. They provide the basis for a more structured approach to appraisal, helping teachers and headteachers to:

- set relevant targets;
- assist in the evaluation of progress;
- identify further development priorities;
- confirm success.

The standards will continue to be kept under review in light both of their use by teachers and headteachers and of emerging national priorities.

Subject Leadership

The *National Standards for Subject Leaders* sets out the knowledge, understanding, skills and attributes which relate to the key areas of subject leadership. The standards define expertise in subject leadership and are designed to guide the professional development of teachers aiming to increase their effectiveness as subject leaders or of those aspiring to take these responsibilities. Most of the standards identified apply equally to other middle managers in schools, e.g. Year Heads, Key Stage Co-ordinators, Advanced Skills Teachers. The standards apply to all schools but will need to be implemented differently in schools of different type, size and phase. For example, they should be used selectively in smaller primary and special schools where headteachers may retain more of the defined roles than in larger primary, special or secondary schools. The degree to which subject (curriculum) co-ordinators in primary and special schools can use the specified knowledge, skills and attributes, in order to carry out the key tasks in these standards, will depend on their experience and the opportunities to develop their role. The standards are based on how experienced and effective co-ordinators provide leadership in their subject(s) or area of work in the school.

Although subject leaders must have a good knowledge of their subject, these standards focus primarily on the expertise in the leadership and management functions. While some aspects of leadership and management are generic, others might be specific to the subject or area of work and the type of school. It is, however, through these generic issues that training and development for subject leadership will provide a good preparation in many of the management and leadership skills for those aspiring to take on broader and more senior leadership and management roles.

The *National Standards for Subject Leaders* is in five parts:

1 Core purpose of the subject leader;
2 Key outcomes of subject leadership;
3 Professional knowledge and understanding;
4 Skills and attributes;
5 Key areas of subject leadership.

The first two elements are dealt with here; the other three form a part of the needs identification exercise in *Supplement P4*.

1 Core Purpose of the Subject Leader

> To provide professional leadership and management for a subject [area] in order to secure high quality teaching, effective use of resources and improved standards of learning and achievement for all pupils.

A subject leader provides leadership and direction for the subject and ensures that it is managed and organised to meet the aims and objectives of the school and the subject (area of work). While the headteacher and governors carry overall responsibility for school improvement, a subject leader has responsibility for securing high standards of teaching and learning in the subject as well as a significant role in the development of whole school policy and practice. Throughout their work, subject leaders ensure that practices improve the quality of education provided, meet the needs and aspirations of the pupils, and raise standards of achievement in the school.

Subject leaders play key roles in supporting, guiding and motivating teachers, support staff and other adults. Subject leaders evaluate the effectiveness of teaching and learning, the curriculum and progress towards targets for pupils and staff, in order to inform future priorities and targets for the subject. The degree to which a subject leader is involved in monitoring, to provide the range of information for evaluation, will depend on school policy and be influenced by the size of the school. Although the subject leader will undertake a variety of monitoring activities, headteachers in smaller primary schools may retain a larger proportion of that monitoring which requires direct classroom observation of teaching and learning. Subject leaders identify the needs in their own subject and recognise that these must be considered in relation to the overall needs of the school. It is important that subject leaders have an understanding of how their subject contributes to school priorities and to the overall education and achievement of all pupils.

2 Key Outcomes of Subject Leadership (the Team's Vision)

Effective subject leadership results in:

- pupils who:

  - show sustained improvement in their knowledge, understanding and skills in relation to prior attainment;
  - understand the key ideas in the subject at a level appropriate to their age and stage of development;
  - show improvement in their literacy, numeracy and information and communications technology skills;
  - know the purpose and sequence of activities;
  - are well prepared for any tests and examinations;
  - are enthusiastic about the subject and highly motivated to continue with their studies;
  - through their attitudes and behaviour, contribute to the maintenance of a purposeful working environment.

- teachers who:

  - work well together as a team;
  - support the aims of the subject (team) and understand how these relate to the school's aims;
  - are involved in the formation of policies and plans and apply them consistently in the classroom;
  - are dedicated to improving standards of teaching and learning;
  - have an enthusiasm for the subject which reinforces the motivation of pupils;
  - have high expectations for the pupils and set realistic but challenging targets based on a good knowledge of their pupils and the progression of concepts in the subject;
  - make good use of guidance, training and support to enhance their knowledge and understanding of the subject and to develop expertise in their teaching;
  - take account of relevant research and inspection findings;
  - make effective use of subject-specific resources;
  - select appropriate teaching and learning approaches to meet subject-specific learning objectives and the needs of the pupils.

- parents who:

  - are well informed about their child's achievements in the subject and about targets for further improvement;

- know the expectations made of their child in learning the subject;
- know how they can support or assist their child's learning in the subject.

- headteachers and other senior managers who:

  - understand the needs of the subject;
  - use information about achievements and development priorities in the subject in order to make well-informed decisions and to achieve greater improvements in the school's development and its aims.

- other adults in the school and community, including technical and administrative staff, classroom assistants, external agencies and representatives of business and industry, who:

  - are informed of subject achievements and priorities;
  - are able, where appropriate, to play an effective role in supporting the teaching and learning.

SUBJECT MANAGEMENT IN SECONDARY SCHOOLS

It is noticeable (OFSTED 1997) that management at all levels in effective and improving schools is co-ordinated to focus on standards in all aspects of the work of the school. The outcomes of such good management practice are evident in the improving quality of teaching and the raising of the levels of pupils' attainments.

The key characteristics of well-managed departments and teams include:

- leadership which is strong but consultative;
- effective and equitable delegation of responsibilities;
- regular and well-managed departmental meetings which enable all staff to contribute to planning and policy making;
- departmental development planning guided by, and contributing to, whole school policies and identifying training and resourcing needs;
- a comprehensive departmental handbook, carrying forward school aims and policies, available for all teachers and including suitable schemes of work for pupils of all ages and abilities;
- systematic monitoring of the quality of teaching and observation of lessons, accompanied by debate about, and sharing of, good practice;
- optimum deployment of staff and effective organisation of teaching groups or classes;
- regular review of teaching and learning resources, and ensuring that all new materials which are acquired provide value for money at all times;
- regular monitoring of the assessment of pupils and moderation of assessments in order to maintain consistency;
- systematic monitoring of the achievement and progress of individual pupils, classes and groups, linked to demanding but realistic target setting and the evaluation of teaching and learning outcomes;
- identification of in-service training needs and opportunities, with appropriate support for new, inexperienced and non-specialist teachers and others with identified weaknesses or areas in need of development or enhancement.

Factors in whole school leadership and management which are necessary for effective middle management are:

- a comprehensive set of school 'aims', enabling middle managers to evaluate their progress, and the progress of their departments or teams, in moving towards them;
- clearly defined roles for teachers and managers at all levels, in particular the responsibilities of senior managers and middle managers for the monitoring of standards and teaching;
- sufficient non-contact time allocated to senior and middle managers to enable them to fulfil their delegated roles effectively;
- a framework for curriculum review with periodic meetings to involve staff in the debate at a range of levels;
- effective whole school development planning, informed by a process of continuous monitoring and review;
- clear guidance about a common structure for schemes of work and departmental handbooks;
- links between a named senior manager and each subject/department;
- whole school policies for assessment, recording and reporting, including homework,

which are implemented and monitored across subjects, departments or year groups;
- systematic use of records of attainment; the use of baseline assessments (benchmarks) to set demanding, but realistic, targets and to monitor progress; heads of department held accountable for external examination performance;
- regular and purposeful monitoring and evaluation of learning and teaching using agreed criteria.

(Adapted from OFSTED 1997)

Planning Processes

DEVELOPMENT PLANNING BY DEPARTMENT/SUBJECT/YEAR GROUP/ KEY STAGE TEAMS

Good planning:

- has a clear focus on raising attainment and promoting pupils' progress by concentrating, as appropriate, on the quality of learning and teaching;
- involves, as appropriate, all the members/partners in the process;
- complements, and is integral to, the school development plan;
- contributes to the continuing process of self-evaluation leading to departmental and school improvement.

The plan should:

- prioritise what needs to be done to raise standards;
- be achievable within a realistic and specified timescale;
- for each issue:

    - state the actions to be addressed;
    - state clear performance indicators, targets and success criteria which will then enable progress in raising standards to be assessed;
    - set appropriate and realistic deadlines;
    - state who will take responsibility;
    - identify arrangements for collecting data and evidence, where appropriate;
    - monitor the progress in implementing the action on the issue;
    - evaluate the effects of the action taken, particularly on pupil attainment and progress;
    - indicate who is responsible for each process and to whom, when and in what form they should report;

- estimate the staff time and cost of any resources needed to implement the plan;
- evolve, in the light of the evaluation processes for the plan.

Proformas

The proformas shown in Tables 3 and 4 are examples of the types that should be used when planning. Proformas should have the following features:

- The same design should be used for all planning processes as this ensures uniformity of approach, increases familiarity with the process and makes the proformas easier to use as working documents throughout the stages of any planning process;
- Brevity, i.e. one side of A4, makes use easier;
- All proformas should be dated at the start of the planning and should also be dated when the 'summary outcome' is completed;
- A copy of each proforma should be filed, preferably in a loose-leaf folder, as this enables easy reference, particularly where developments have to be extended or lead on to other related initiatives.

Table 3 Development planning proforma for team/department/year group

Team/Group:	Date:
Issue for development (relate to School Development, OFSTED Action Plan as appropriate)	
Development, implementation and monitoring strategies to be used	
Specific performance indicators and success criteria or targets	
Start and anticipated end dates	
Training implications	
Estimated costs (time and finance)	Actual costs
Anticipated effects on whole school, other depts/year groups	
Evaluation strategies (related to performance indicators/success criteria or targets above)	
Summary outcome (including consideration of next steps) Date:	

Table 4 Action planning proforma as used by one primary school for all planning at school and
subject levels

Initiative:		Date:			
Aims:					
Intended outcomes:		Success criteria:			
Staff responsible:		Others involved:			
Start Date:	End Date:	Number of school days/weeks:			
Action to be taken		Start date	End date	Cost	Budget
INSET needs:					
Issues arising:					

ANALYSING COMPLEX ISSUES: THE ART OF DIAGRAMMING

The inclusion of this supplement is based on four assertions backed by a number of studies (e.g. Open University 1986) showing that maps are a more effective means of conveying complex data issues than text:

- Planning, particularly for change, is often complex and is characterised by a large number of interacting elements operating both inside and outside the school/department/year group/team;
- In oral discussion and description there is greater difficulty in handling such complexity; a diagram can aid understanding by providing not only a 'mind-map' of the interrelationships but also a model of what currently exists and what might be added or put in its place;
- Proposals for change are often complex and using diagrams can help to communicate ideas within the team or to senior managers before the final document or policy is produced;
- Using diagrams which conform to one convention can help to clarify ideas in a way that *ad hoc* sketches might not.

The process is best done using a whiteboard or flip-chart and can be a 'brainstorming' activity by a group or an individual. It is sometimes valuable for the team leader to have already produced the first strands, which are often the easiest. This helps to save time, in that others quickly get involved with the more detailed aspects and can often add to the main branches of the diagram. The involvement of the team gives an excellent opportunity for developing ownership of the issues at an early stage and this usually carries over to the more detailed development later.

The example given in Figure 3 was a first attempt by a group of middle managers working with a deputy head. The impetus for considering the issue was a potential budget deficit which was affecting the finance available for departmental resources. As with most diagramming activities it went far beyond the original intention and began considering all aspects of funds outside the school budget and then the wider range of purposes for which the funds raised might be used. The group realised that there were legal implications for many of the aspects they had included (e.g. charging policy, liability, VAT), on which they would need advice.

Having covered most aspects of fund raising, the group then intended to select one area from the map and to repeat the process in greater detail, i.e. use the mind-mapping exercise to take the analysis a step further.

As management tools, maps should:

- help people to understand the present situation;
- help to clarify the desired situation;
- show clearly the interrelationships between the various aspects of the issue being considered;
- suggest means of moving from one part to another (this approach is used extensively in schools in the development of 'work-webs' to show the interrelating elements within a topic);

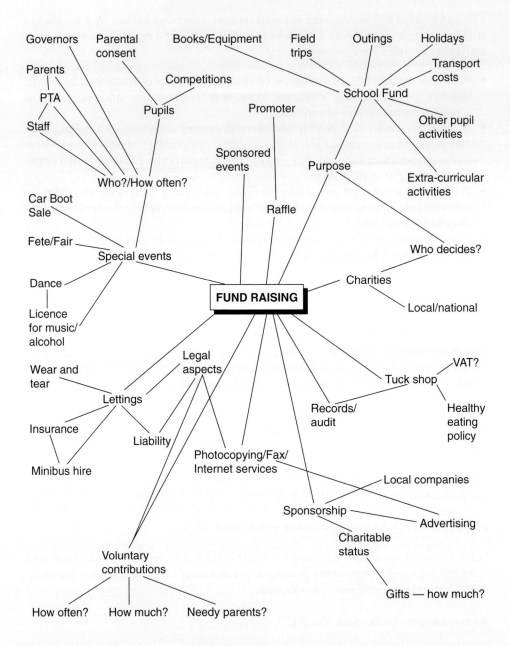

Figure 3 An example of a completed mapping exercise

- help to clarify the thinking of individuals and groups;
- provide opportunities for sharing within the team;
- provide a rapid, first phase of planning.

The general principles governing the use of diagramming are:

- the process is neither difficult nor easy but, as with most planning processes, techniques improve with practice;
- diagrams can be maps showing relationships in space or time, or logical diagrams showing how the parts depend upon each other;
- diagrams are 'holistic' in that they usually give a much better understanding of, and feeling for, the issues than a large quantity of text and/or talk;
- understanding of the issue tends to grow as it is expressed in diagrammatic form;
- it is rare to get everything right at the first attempt; skill in laying out a diagram develops with practice;
- it is better to develop a common convention for the form of the diagram and use it regularly.

When the diagram is complete, it should be used to identify:

- the action to be taken (it is advisable to concentrate on only a small part at a time and not to be over-ambitious);
- any of the linking parts which might be included;
- who and what might be involved;
- when action should be taken.

PLANNING AND MANAGEMENT OF CHANGE

Research has shown that most teachers take a pragmatic view of their responsibilities as teachers. They tend to answer the following questions intuitively, to determine what it is desirable and possible to teach, and then start their planning:

- What am I going to teach in this lesson and how does this relate to the departmental/subject scheme of work?
- How does this lesson link to the previous lessons and is there a need to recap or repeat any part of it?
- What do I expect the pupils to learn during this lesson and have they any prior learning on this topic?
- Have I taught this topic to a class/group before and, if so, what were the strengths and weaknesses then?
- What is the range of ability and are there any pupils with special educational needs, including the most able pupils?
- Have equal opportunities issues been addressed?
- What are the pupils' likely interests, motivation and behaviour?
- What assessment opportunities will be available?
- What is the attendance and where are the 'absent' pupils, if any?
- Is the classroom and its layout appropriate and are the necessary resources available?
- How will the lesson time be divided to allow for a variety of teaching strategies and learning approaches to be used?
- Will the time of the day, week and term have any influence on the way the lesson/topic is taught and on the anticipated outcomes?
- What would be appropriate homework tasks and is there homework to be collected in and/or set?
- What problems are anticipated and are there strategies to deal with these?

However, in managing or preparing for change it is necessary for teachers to extend this approach, as they are the main agents through which improvements in pupils' achievement are made and standards are raised. Unfortunately, many teachers find change stressful and difficult to accept and they sometimes feel threatened. This has not been helped by the period of rapid, and sometimes repetitive, change that has been imposed in recent years.

Any change, such as the introduction of a new element in the teaching programmes, will require some or all of the following from teachers:

- additional time;
- acceptance of new ideas and the learning of new skills;
- change in teaching methodologies and styles;
- collaboration with colleagues which may necessitate some loss of professional independence and a perceived undermining of their subject experience and expertise;
- dependence on the expertise and competence of others;
- sharing of ideas and resources;
- loss of confidence and perhaps effectiveness in the short term.

Initially, any change for the sake of improvement will be embraced by those teachers who:

- feel that change is necessary;
- are highly motivated;
- believe that they are personally accountable;
- are eager to accept the notion of continuous professional development.

The teachers who are resistant to change are characterised by their preferring to:

- focus their energies only on the current lesson or series of lessons;
- avoid working with other teachers;
- avoid planning beyond the end of their current teaching commitment;
- remain in their comfortable, known position and avoid new challenges.

The behaviour of some teachers throughout a lifelong teaching career follows a pattern, namely initial enthusiasm, growth in self-confidence, gradual self-development, increasing boredom, a feeling of isolation, characteristic cynicism, non-involvement. It is of vital importance to break this pattern if team/departmental improvement is to be maintained and standards of pupils' work are to be raised. This can be achieved through relevant, appropriate and interesting staff development. The truism that, in order to be effective, lifelong teachers need to accept that they must be lifelong learners has, in part, been borne out by the way in which most teachers have adapted to the use of ICT in their teaching and administrative work.

IDENTIFYING PERSONAL, TEAM OR DEPARTMENTAL DEVELOPMENT NEEDS

The *National Standards for Subject Leaders*, published by the Teacher Training Agency in 1998 and outlined in *Supplement KE3*, forms a valuable basis for a needs identification framework for both middle managers and those teachers aspiring to such responsibilities. In addition, the framework below can be used, in part, as a supplement for an audit of the stage of any development planning that the team or department intends to undertake.

The list of issues on pp. 95–101 is comprehensive and it is unlikely that all parts would be attempted at the same time unless there were to be a complete review of all team/departmental policies. However, it is ideal if used as an audit and a means to identify needs whenever a particular aspect is being planned or reviewed.

It can be used collectively by teams/departments or individually, followed by an 'airing, sharing and comparing' of the team's views. Both approaches are good exercises for testing team/departmental consensus, or lack of it!

The Task

Use the boxes, labelled 1 to 3, in the lists on pp. 95–101 to make an assessment of the existing levels of experience, expertise or development. This may be done either as a self-assessment by the team leader/middle manager or as a collective assessment by the team/department.

Key	Personal need	Team/Departmental need
1	Confident on this issue, have experience and knowledge	Policy/procedure already in place and working well
2	Some knowledge and experience, not priority need at present	In place but in need of revision/review at some stage
3	Limited or no experience in this area – need for professional development	Policy/procedure not developed or implemented, a priority area of need

Subject leaders should have knowledge and understanding of:	1	2	3
• their school's aims, priorities, targets and action plans			
• the relationship of the subject to the curriculum as a whole			
• any statutory curriculum requirements for the subject and the requirements for assessment, recording and reporting of pupils' attainment and progress			
• the characteristics of high quality teaching in the subject and the main strategies for improving and sustaining high standards of teaching, learning and achievement for all pupils			
• how evidence from relevant research, inspection evidence and local, national and international standards of achievement can be used to inform expectations, targets and teaching approaches			
• how to use comparative data, together with information about pupils' prior attainment, to establish benchmarks and to set targets for improvement			
• how to develop pupils' literacy, numeracy and information and communications technology skills through the subject			
• how teaching the subject can promote pupils' spiritual, moral, social, cultural, mental and physical development			
• management, including employment law, equal opportunities legislation, personnel, external relations, finance and change			
• how teaching the subject can help to prepare pupils for the opportunities, responsibilities and experiences of adult life			
• the current use and future potential of information and communications technology to aid teaching and learning of the subject, and to assist with subject management			
• the role of school governance and how it can contribute to the work of the subject leader			
• the implications of information and guidance documents from LEAs, the DfEE, QCA, TTA, OFSTED and other national bodies and associations			
• the implications of the Code of Practice for Special Educational Needs for teaching and learning in their subject			
• health and safety requirements, including where to obtain expert advice			

Skills and attributes

- Leadership skills, attributes and professional competence – the ability to lead and manage people to work towards common goals

Where other staff teach or support the subject, subject leaders should be able to:	I	2	3
• secure commitment to a clear aim and direction for the subject			
• prioritise, plan and organise			
• work as a part of a team			
• deal sensitively with people, recognise individual needs and take account of these in securing a consistent team approach to raising achievement in the subject			
• acknowledge and use the experience, expertise and contribution of others			
• set standards and provide a role model for pupils and other staff in the teaching and learning of the subject			
• devolve responsibilities and delegate tasks, as appropriate			
• seek advice and support when necessary.			

Subject leaders should have the professional competence and expertise to:	I	2	3
• command credibility through the discharge of their duties and use their expertise to influence others in relation to the subject			
• make informed use of research and inspection findings			
• apply good practice to and from other subject areas			

- Decision-making skills – the ability to solve problems and make decisions

Subject leaders should be able to:	I	2	3
• judge when to make decisions, when to consult with others, and when to defer to the headteacher or senior managers			
• analyse, understand and interpret relevant information and data			
• think creatively and imaginatively to anticipate and to solve problems and identify opportunities			

- Communication skills – the ability to make points clearly and understand the views of others

Subject leaders should be able to:	I	2	3
• communicate effectively, orally and in writing, with the headteacher, other staff, pupils, parents, governors, external agencies and the wider community, including business and industry			
• negotiate and consult effectively			
• ensure good communication with, and between, staff who teach and support the subject			
• chair meetings effectively			

- Self-management – the ability to plan time effectively and to organise oneself well

Subject leaders should be able to:	I	2	3
• prioritise and manage their own time effectively, particularly in relation to balancing the demands made by teaching, subject management and involvement in school development			
• achieve challenging professional goals			
• take responsibility for their own professional development			

- Attributes

Subject leaders draw upon:	I	2	3
• personal impact and presence			
• adaptability to changing circumstances and new ideas			
• energy, vigour and perseverance			
• self-confidence			
• enthusiasm			
• intellectual ability			
• reliability and integrity			
• commitment			

Key areas of subject leadership

A range of leadership and management tasks is set out on pp. 98–101 for each of the key areas of subject leadership:

- Strategic direction and development of the subject
- Teaching and learning
- Leading and managing staff
- Efficient and effective deployment of staff and resources

Expertise in subject leadership is demonstrated by the ability to apply professional knowledge, understanding, skills and attributes to the identified tasks in order to bring about the desired outcomes.

Strategic direction and development of the subject

Within the context of the school's aims and policies, subject leaders develop and implement subject policies, plans, targets and practices.

Subject Leaders:	1	2	3
• develop and implement policies and practices for the subject which reflect the school's commitment to high achievement, effective teaching and learning			
• create a climate which enables other staff to develop and maintain positive attitudes towards the subject and confidence in teaching it			
• establish a clear, shared understanding of the importance of and role of the subject in contributing to pupils' spiritual, moral, cultural, mental and physical development, and in preparing pupils for the opportunities, responsibilities and experiences of adult life			
• use data effectively to identify pupils who are underachieving in the subject and, where necessary, create and implement effective plans of action to support those pupils			
• analyse and interpret relevant national, local and school data, plus research and inspection evidence, in order to inform policies, practices, expectations, targets and teaching methods			
• establish, with the involvement of relevant staff, short-, medium- and long-term plans for the development and resourcing of the subject, which:			
– contribute to whole school aims, policies and practices, including those in relation to behaviour, discipline, bullying and racial harassment			
– are based on a range of comparative information and evidence, including in relation to the attainment of pupils			
– identify realistic and challenging targets for improvement in the subject			
– are understood by all those involved in putting the plans into practice			
– are clear about action to be taken, timescales and criteria for success			
• monitor the progress made in achieving subject plans and targets, evaluate the effects on teaching and learning and use this analysis to guide further improvement			

Teaching and learning

Subject leaders secure and sustain effective teaching of the subject, evaluate the quality of teaching and standards of pupil achievements and set targets for improvement.

Subject Leaders:	1	2	3
• ensure curriculum coverage, continuity and progression in the subject for all pupils, including those of high ability and those with special educational or linguistic needs			
• ensure that teachers are clear about the teaching objectives in lessons, understand the sequence of teaching and learning in the subject, and communicate such information to pupils			
• provide guidance on the choice of appropriate teaching and learning methods to meet the needs of the subject and of different pupils			
• ensure effective development of pupils' literacy, numeracy and information and communications technology skills through the subject			
• establish and implement clear policies and practices for assessing, recording and reporting on pupil achievement, and for using this information to recognise achievement and to assist pupils in setting targets for further improvement			
• ensure that information about pupils' achievements in previous classes and schools is used effectively to secure good progress in the subject			
• set expectations and targets for staff and pupils in relation to the standards of pupil achievement and the quality of teaching, and evaluate progress and achievement in the subject by all pupils, including those with special educational or linguistic needs			
• evaluate the teaching of the subject in the school, use this analysis to identify effective practice and areas for improvement, and take action to improve further the quality of teaching			
• ensure effective development of pupils' individual and collaborative study skills which are necessary for them to become increasingly independent in their work and to complete tasks independently when out of school			
• ensure that teachers of the subject are aware of its contribution to pupils' understanding of the duties, opportunities, responsibilities and rights of citizens			
• ensure that teachers of the subject know how to recognise and deal with racial stereotyping			
• establish a partnership with parents to involve them in their child's learning of the subject, as well as providing information about curriculum, attainment, progress and targets			
• develop effective links with the local community, including business and industry, in order to extend the subject curriculum, to enhance teaching and to develop pupils' wider understanding			

Leading and managing staff

Subject leaders provide, to all those with an involvement in the teaching or support of the subject, the support, challenge, information and development necessary to sustain motivation and secure improvement in teaching.

Subject Leaders:	I	2	3
• help staff to achieve constructive working relationships with pupils			
• establish clear expectations and constructive working relationships among staff involved in the subject (e.g. through team working and mutual support); devolving responsibilities and delegating tasks, as appropriate; evaluating practice; and developing an acceptance of accountability			
• sustain their own motivation and, where possible, that of other staff involved in the subject			
• appraise staff as required by the school policy and use the process to develop the personal and professional effectiveness of the appraisee(s)			
• audit training needs of subject staff			
• lead professional development of subject staff through example and support, and co-ordinate the provision of high quality professional development by methods such as coaching, drawing on other sources of expertise as necessary (e.g. higher education, LEAs, subject associations)			
• ensure that trainee and newly qualified teachers are appropriately trained, monitored, supported and assessed in relation to standards for the award of Qualified Teacher Status, the Career Entry Profiles and standards for induction			
• enable teachers to achieve expertise in their subject teaching			
• work with the SENCO and any other staff with special educational needs expertise in order to ensure that individual education plans are used to set subject-specific targets and match work well to the pupils' needs			
• ensure that the headteacher, senior managers and governors are well informed about subject policies, plans and priorities, the success in meeting the objectives and targets, and subject-related professional development plans			

Efficient and effective deployment of staff and resources
Subject leaders identify appropriate resources for the subject and ensure that they are used efficiently, effectively and safely.

Subject Leaders:	1	2	3
• establish staff and resource needs for the subject and advise the headteacher and senior managers of likely priorities for expenditure, and allocate available subject resources with maximum efficiency in order to meet the objectives of the school and of subject plans and to achieve value for money			
• deploy, or advise the headteacher on the deployment of, staff involved in the subject to ensure the best use of subject, technical and other expertise			
• ensure the effective and efficient management and organisation of learning resources, including information and communications technology			
• maintain existing resources and explore possibilities to develop or incorporate new resources from a wide variety of sources inside and outside the school			
• use accommodation to create an effective and stimulating environment for the teaching and learning of the subject			
• ensure that there is a safe working and learning environment in which risks are properly assessed			

Once the lists have been completed there is a need to prioritise those areas which have been identified as category 3, i.e. in greatest need of development. However, where this is a team exercise, there would also be a need to agree on the priorities before deciding on the best action to take. Whether the exercise is done by an individual or by a team, there must also be a limit to the number of issues that can be tackled, i.e. ambition and targets must be realistic and attainable. Once a top priority has been established, the issue should then go through the development planning process described in Part 1 and in *Supplement P1*.

THE USE OF PERFORMANCE INDICATORS TO ESTABLISH SUCCESS CRITERIA

Identifying performance indicators is an essential part of any development planning process. They are by definition indicators and not measures in themselves. They are used to identify and establish the success criteria, the measurable elements, by which the effectiveness of new initiatives/plans are to be evaluated. The criteria selected should be measurable or should provide evidence on which a professional judgement can be made. They should be few in number and should be specific, to allow for accurate assessment of success (or lack of it) rather than relying on the 'feel good factor' approach which in the past has too often been used to indicate improvement. The lists on pp. 102–13 are categorised under the various aspects of planning that middle managers have to undertake. From these lists middle managers or teams should select items which they will use as indicators of present performance to be compared with new targets to be set in the plan. Many of the indicators are quantifiable but others will need to be used to provide the evidence for professional judgements to be made. Examples of these judgements are the performance indicators for assessing the quality of teaching and learning, which are used in OFSTED inspections and are given in *Supplement TL1*.

Leadership and Management of Staff

Issues

- Leadership and management of both teaching and support staff consists in large measure of ensuring the most economic, effective and efficient deployment of the human resources available. This must be directed towards the achievement of the best possible quality of teaching and learning and thereby the highest possible achievement by the pupils.
- The styles of leadership and management must take into account the staff concerned, individuals and groups, and the context of the situation.

Indicators

- Professional qualifications, curricular experience and expertise:

    - experience and present level of appointment;
    - teachers' qualifications;
    - match of teaching commitments to qualifications and expertise;
    - recent and relevant professional development;
    - course and lesson planning;

- Effectiveness of communication:

    - within the team;
    - with the school management team and governors
    - with other departments and teams;
    - with pupils, both in and out of the classroom;
    - with parents;
    - with the community;
    - with other external individuals, agencies or groups;

- Documentation

  - job descriptions;
  - teaching programmes;
  - pupil records, including assessments, benchmarks and targets;
  - pupil reports;
  - use of schemes of work and lesson plans;
  - compliance with agreed deadlines;
  - references on staff (open or closed?);

- Attributes:

  - personal impact and presence;
  - adaptability to changing circumstances and new ideas;
  - energy, vigour and perseverance;
  - self-confidence;
  - enthusiasm;
  - intellectual ability;
  - reliability and integrity;
  - commitment.

Quality of Teaching

Issues

- The quality of teaching is almost inseparable from the quality of learning. Hence, the central indicators of successful teaching must be related to the outcomes for the pupils. Factors such as client/stakeholder satisfaction are also clearly relevant.
- The quality of good teaching and learning can be found in a variety of, often contradictory, contexts where the quality is mostly intangible, associated with the personalities of teacher and pupils and the relationships between them.

Indicators

- Management and organisation of time and the deployment of staff:

  - teaching loads;
  - deployment according to experience and special expertise, abilities and skills;
  - management of teaching time and conditions of service;

- Effectiveness of teaching:

  - secure command of the subject and courses, the National Curriculum and its assessment;
  - clear and appropriate goals in the context of well-planned, overt schemes of work;
  - pupils are clear about what, why, how, how long and the standards expected;
  - lessons are well planned and have suitable and relevant content;
  - pupils are well managed, ensuring high standards of behaviour and self-discipline;
  - pupils are engaged and motivated;
  - clear exposition and varied use of questioning with strategic recaps;

- frequent use of praise;
- high expectations of self and pupils;
- suitable pace and differentiation (by task and outcome), with support for less able and demanding targets for the more able;
- well-organised groupings;
- effective use and organisation of relevant resources;
- appropriate assessment and recording strategies;
- selection and use of appropriate teaching styles and strategies;
- appropriate homework to reinforce and/or extend learning;

• Achievement of targets:

- assessment including marking (diagnosis, feedback, remediation);
- work load distribution (contact ratios, group sizes, timetables);
- equal opportunity issues – age, gender, ethnicity, special needs.

Quality of Relationships

Effectiveness of Communications

Effectiveness of communications to and from the head (and governors where appropriate) and the school management team, other teams/departments and support staff:

• with staff:

- delegation (empowerment) and acceptance of responsibility;
- teamwork;
- initiative;
- trust;

• with pupils:

- discipline (work and behaviour);
- awareness of individual needs;
- support and guidance;
- sympathy;
- humour (fun!);

• with parents:

- tact;
- confidentiality;
- awareness of their differing circumstances and levels of understanding;
- friendliness;
- support.

Commitment and professional attitudes

• commitment;
• dedication;
• conscientiousness;
• extra-curricular involvement;
• attendance;

- punctuality;
- liaison with governors, parents, other schools, FE/HE, the 'world of work'.

Quality of Learning

Issues

- Pupils' learning is too often assumed to be indicated purely by their performance in relation to easily quantified measures (e.g. results in tests, examinations and other standardised tests). Whilst these are obviously important, they do not of course tell the whole story. Achievement can be demonstrated and assessed in many areas which are not, and which quite properly should not be, the subject of such formal assessment.
- Although quantifiable indicators of outcomes of learning are crucial, it is also possible (and necessary) to consider the learning process, and the nature and quality of the whole of the educational experience. Is the pupils' learning effective in that it is related to their individual needs and capabilities and begins to prepare them for the opportunities, responsibilities and experiences of adult life? These general considerations of the purposes for learning are invariably included in school aims or mission statements and they provide the essential backcloth for the range of indicators suggested below.

Indicators

Quality of curricular management

- Research and policy:
  - curriculum offered and its relation to the National Curriculum and whole school and LEA policies/guidelines;
  - programmes of study, syllabuses, schemes of work, lesson plans;
  - benchmarking and target setting;
  - syllabuses used in Key Stage 4 and sixth form;
  - take-up of subject as an option as a whole, and by boys and girls;
  - organisation – streaming, banding, setting, mixed ability, 'fast tracking', etc.;
  - publication of information on options and market research;
  - examination entry;
  - use of link courses;
  - relevant work experience and uptake, links with local 'world of work';
  - use of field studies, extra-curricular and out of school activities;

- Implementation:
  - breadth, balance, coherence and progression;
  - equal opportunities and access;
  - cross-curricular elements, particularly literacy, numeracy and ICT;
  - spiritual, moral, social and cultural development;

- Review and evaluation:
  - analysis and development;

- differentiation;
- pupils with linguistic and other special educational needs.

Management of time

- Timetabling:

  - analysis;
  - clarity, structure and layout;
  - taught hours;
  - teaching lesson lengths and distribution;
  - appropriateness of teaching groups (sizes, streaming, banding, setting, etc.).

- Pupils' programmes:

  - use of time;
  - balance;
  - coherence;
  - relevance and responsiveness to individual needs and aspirations.

Engagement in the learning process

- attitudes and behaviour; relationships, pupil to pupil and pupil to teacher;
- motivation, interest, degree of attention and responsiveness;
- concentration, perseverance, enthusiasm and excitement;
- initiative, enquiry, research;
- problem-solving;
- response to challenge, initiative shown, work independently and productively without close supervision;
- observing, posing questions, seeking information, using and applying learning in new contexts;
- search for patterns and deeper understanding;
- evidence of understanding and retention;
- individual work, participation and co-operation in groups;
- selection and handling of materials and equipment;
- variety of learning strategies and resources;
- talk, discuss and listen;
- writing in a variety of styles appropriate to tasks;
- practical activities;
- communication, modification and evaluation of work done.

Breadth and quality of the learning experience

- knowledge;
- conceptual understanding;
- learning related to needs;
- suitable level of task;
- curricular range and balance;
- coherence;
- continuity and progression;

- relevance and durability;
- values: social, moral, ethical and spiritual.

Outcomes of learning

- records of achievement, individual educational plans;
- personal, social and cultural development;
- literacy: reading, writing, listening and speaking;
- numeracy;
- information and communications technology;
- scientific understanding;
- graphicacy;
- aesthetic development;
- creativity;
- moral, ethical and spiritual development;
- attitudes to work, other people and society;
- attainment and achievement measures, including tests, public examinations, other standardised tests and records of achievement;
- value added measures and their use at school and subject levels;
- destinations of school leavers.

Quality of Homework

Issues

- Whilst homework is clearly a part of the quality of both learning and teaching, it is identified separately as it generates some of its own indicators.
- There is now an even more widespread, though not universal, acceptance of the belief that good homework practice is associated with higher levels of pupil achievement, particularly with older pupils. Although this has rarely been investigated systematically, there is some research evidence (see *Homework*, DfEE 1998) which supports this belief.
- If for no other reason than that the additional time devoted to studies ought to contribute towards higher standards, it is worth looking at possible indicators of successful policy and practice in setting and assessing homework.

Indicators

Policies

- Statements for:

  - staff – generic whole school and subject-specific;
  - pupils;
  - parents;
  - governors;

- If such statements already exist, are they up to date, accepted and implemented?

Scope

- reasons for setting homework and relation to the school aims;
- implementation procedures;
- methods of setting, collecting, assessing and recording;
- variety and appropriateness of tasks in relation to subject;
- recommended time: year group and ability related (per day/week and time-scale for completion);
- spread of homework to account for effective completion and marking;
- feedback to pupils (and parents);
- use of school time, lunchtime and before or after school provision.

Practice

Nature of homework tasks:

- relationship to classwork;
- extension and/or reinforcement work;
- clarity of objectives;
- use of out of school environments;
- independence, research and initiative;
- co-operation with parents and the community areas affected;
- differential effect of pupils' home settings.

Conditions for success

- expectations for pupils and staff;
- commitment;
- realistic time allocation (intention and reality!);
- use of school premises (and staff?) in breaks and before or after school;
- parental agreement and commitment;
- monitoring and evaluation by team leader, or member of school management team, to ensure practice matches policy in terms of quantity set and quality achieved.

Outcomes

- quality of completed homework;
- reception of work, marking, assessment and grading;
- feedback, positive reinforcement;
- rewards and sanctions.

Quality of Guidance (Personal and Social Development and Health Education)

Issues

- Whilst accepting that guidance is a responsibility for *all* staff in all aspects of school life, most schools have deployed staff to special responsibilities for guidance although it is significant that guidance now relates to all facets of a pupil's life in school.

- For this reason, indicators of successful 'pastoral care' overlap with, and repeat, many of the indicators already listed in the quality of learning and teaching and for homework.

Indicators

- Pastoral management:

    - staffing structures, responsibilities and training;
    - involvement of, and with, the school management team;
    - provision and use of tutorial time;
    - monitoring academic progress;
    - personal and social development programmes;
    - use of senior pupils: responsibilities, monitoring and training;
    - accommodation for assemblies, tutorial and social activities, pastoral managers and staff;
    - year group and/or school councils;

- Expectations:

    - aims, guidelines and schemes of work;
    - review procedures;
    - monitoring and evaluation of programmes;
    - meetings of pastoral staff teams;

- Tutorial arrangements:

    - registration procedures and use of registration time;
    - provision and use of tutorial time;
    - relationships: pupil to pupil and pupils to teacher;
    - response and attitudes of pupils;

- Guidance and counselling:

    - educational guidance and liaison with heads of department or subject and other members of the teams;
    - vocational guidance and links with careers programmes;
    - liaison with careers teachers and careers officers;
    - personal guidance and liaison with parents;
    - counselling and links with external agencies and the 'world of work';

- Attendance and punctuality:

    - attendance and punctuality patterns of individuals and groups;
    - monitoring of attendance;
    - follow-up procedures and links with welfare agencies;

- Privileges, rewards and sanctions:

    - range of rewards and privileges, use of records of achievement;
    - range of sanctions, their monitoring and effectiveness;
    - suspensions and exclusions (temporary and permanent);
    - involvement of parents;

- Corporate activities:

    - assemblies, year group and form group meetings;

- other formal and informal organisation and planning;
- extra-curricular activities and competitions;
- pupils' participation rates in activities;
- opportunities for responsibilities across all year groups;
- democratic structures (e.g. year group or school councils);

- Attitudes and behaviour:

  - agreed and accepted code of behaviour;
  - evidence of self-discipline;
  - recognition of positive attitudes and good behaviour;
  - records of unacceptable behaviour;
  - incidence of vandalism, in and out of school hours;
  - incidence of graffiti, damage and litter.

Financial Management

Issues

- Costs per pupil are useful indicators of financial performance both within the subject area/year group and across the departments/year groups in the whole school. They can highlight areas requiring further investigation and review.
- Unit costs generally represent input measures rather than process or output measures. However, they do allow for comparisons and judgements to be made but should not be used in isolation without reference to other indicators.
- Unit costs also allow for year on year comparisons as well as the relative costs for pupils of different ages, e.g. where there is a sixth form, to what extent is the provision being subsidised at the expense of the main school pupils (some of whom will not stay on to benefit from this subsidy)?
- The introduction of financial management by schools, and recent stringent spending controls, has required much more careful control over spending but does allow schools to make the large majority of their own financial decisions. This has given rise to the need for:

  - full, accurate and up-to-date financial records of resource allocation and spending;
  - a more careful analysis of spending in all areas;
  - much more careful book-keeping and monitoring systems;
  - a striving for economy, efficiency and effectiveness, i.e. value for money;
  - accountability.

- These same principles should operate in all of the departments and year groups where separate finance is provided. The detail of departmental expenditure may, however, be maintained on the school's Management Information System (MIS) which, as long as this information is easily and readily accessible, may suffice for departmental/year group use.

Indicators

- Fully costed subject, department or year group development plan;
- Financial records showing evidence of:

- all spending;
- justified carry-over;
- levels of spending on the aspects shown below under 'costs per pupil';
- level of funding from sources other than the school budget;
- parental contributions (see *Charging Policy*, p. 65);
- shortfall over identified need;

- Costs per pupil for:

  - teaching staff;
  - support staff;
  - books (texts and library books), materials and equipment;
  - repairs, maintenance, contracts and insurance;
  - off-site provision (e.g. link courses, use of leisure centres);
  - other costs per pupil;

- Reprographics, stationery, postage and telephone;
- Extra-curricular and out of school activities (see *Charging Policy*, p. 65);
- Transport costs;
- Use and costs of external agencies/support (e.g. LEA staff, music, dance and drama specialists and companies);
- Use of centrally held library and computer resources.

Liaison with Parents

Issues

- Research has shown that parents' direct involvement with the school has positive effects on the pupils' attitudes and levels of achievement (see *Home–School Agreements: Guidance for Schools*, DfEE 1998).
- This is governed by the school's attempts to keep all parents interested, well informed and, wherever possible, involved in the day-to-day life and activities of the school.
- There are seven broad areas of activity relating to parental involvement which have proved effective:

  - the information available to parents;
  - opportunities for meeting staff, pupils and other parents;
  - participation in the formal activities, in school and at home;
  - involvement in extra-curricular and other out of school activities;
  - opportunities for informal contacts;
  - the availability of the school for use by the parents;
  - the attitudes of the parents towards the school and its work.

Indicators

- The information available to parents:

  - statutory information (see *Reporting*, p. 34);
  - inspection reports;
  - the school calendar;
  - the lesson and homework timetables;

- newsletters;
- reports of positive pupil achievement and endeavour;
- instances of concern about pupils before problems become more serious;
- opportunities for individuals to seek advice and ask questions;
- parent governor involvement in information seeking and distribution;

- Opportunities to meet staff and other parents:

  - a variety of meetings, formal and informal, with individuals, groups and social meetings and events;
  - welcoming atmosphere with refreshments to 'break the ice';
  - use of a translator where the parents' first language is not English;

- Participation in the work of the school:

  - opportunities to be involved in the formal work (e.g. parents with special experience and/or expertise, parent/pupil reading schemes, helping pupils with special education needs, classroom support);
  - advice on how to help with homework tasks;
  - help with out of school and extra-curricular activities, school trips, etc.;
  - parent–school liaison schemes;

- Use of the school by parents:

  - a pleasant welcome and a comfortable, private waiting area;
  - a notice board for use by parents;
  - arrangements to supply translations of important documentation;
  - availability of the school (free of charge?) for meetings of parents and for their sporting, leisure and social activities;

- Attitudes of parents towards the school:

  - active parent/teacher association, parents' association, 'Friends of the School', etc.;
  - level of attendance at annual parents' meeting, year group parents' evenings, school presentation and performance evenings;
  - level of interest in PTA events and in extra-curricular and out of school activities.

Liaison with other Schools/Colleges, the Community and other Agencies

Issues

- The effectiveness of a two-way communication and the quality of relationships are of great importance if the 'external' groups are to become, and to feel, true partners in the work of the school, subject, department or year group.
- This involves providing, for the other 'stakeholders', the best service as well as wanting the best, in terms of help and support.
- Where the school has community provision, issues such as the impact and possible benefits of dual use of accommodation and equipment, client satisfaction, and the involvement of those running the community programmes are significant.

Indicators

- The time and opportunities given to inform the 'external partners' of the work of the subject, department, year group or class;
- Attempts made to publicise and market the work of the department, year group or class;
- Involvement in school activities – presentation and open evenings, performances, careers evenings, extra-curricular and out of school activities, etc.;
- Links with local industry and commercial companies, work experience, teacher placements and secondments from industry to the school;
- Sponsorships.

IMPLEMENTATION OF NEW INITIATIVES

In order to carry through a 'policy' for a new initiative or a change in practice, it is important to ensure that there is a clear framework for implementation. This avoids the danger of assuming that the completion of a written policy is an end point in itself. As with any stage in the planning process it is vital that the mission and vision of the team underpin any action taken:

- There needs to be positive leadership for the initiative, not necessarily by the team leader in every instance;
- Members of the team have to be aware of the role of the 'leader' and their responsibilities within the plan for the new initiative;
- There must be a team commitment to the plan/initiative;
- Any new plan, or phases within it, should have clear objectives including success criteria/performance indicators which are measurable or about which informed judgements can be made;
- The objectives should also have deadlines which are known to all of the team;
- Resource allocation of finance, materials (where appropriate), staff and time must be adequate;
- The deadlines and resource requirements should be monitored and revised, if necessary, at intervals during the implementation phase;
- During the implementation phase members of the team should make a note of the benefits, gains and improvements as well as any difficulties, errors and omissions;
- The leader may have to intervene regularly with suggestions, encouragement, support and help.

There must be constant monitoring/reviewing during the implementation phase. Where progress is slow (or stops) there should be a review of the plan in order to consider the reasons why this has happened:

- were the goals realistic?
- was the timescale appropriate?
- was there sufficient resource allocation?
- were the team sufficiently committed to the plan?
- was the leadership appropriate and adequate?
- were the outcomes congruent with the team's mission and vision?

Unless these points are resolved there will be only frustration and yet another plan will be forgotten and left to gather dust.

EVALUATION OF SCHOOL AND DEPARTMENTAL INITIATIVES

P
7

Questions asked at the evaluation stage of the planning process need to be precise, avoiding the possibility of simply using the 'feel good factor' as evidence for improvement or, even worse, not attempting to question the process and outcomes. The questions which need to be answered are:

- Do we know exactly how much of what we intended to achieve has been accomplished, i.e. have we matched the outcomes to the success criteria and the performance indicators we identified?
- To what extent have we met the success criteria?
- If the success criteria were not met, did we:

  - use the wrong performance indicators?
  - use over-ambitious success criteria?
  - give too little time/finance?

- Do we know whether our planning has improved the quality of the pupils' learning and the standards they are achieving?
- In the light of our experience and reflective judgement, were the priorities we chose the right ones and do we need to adjust our list of priorities for the rest of the time span in our development plan?
- As a result of our evaluation, are we clear about:

  - the success of the strategies we used to attain our targets?
  - the realism of the timescale we set ourselves?
  - the costs in terms of human effort and other tasks not done?
  - what we need to do next?

- Have we acknowledged the value of any unexpected effects (beneficial and detrimental) we could not have predicted, e.g. gains in the commitment, professional competence and confidence of the staff?
- Have we taken the opportunity to enhance our own evaluation of the improvements by incorporating the views of others, e.g. OFSTED, the LEA, the parents, the pupils?
- What lessons have been learned which may improve our next planning activity?
- Have we published the findings of our evaluation, acknowledging the progress made and confirming which areas need more work?
- Have we achieved our improvements economically and efficiently as well as effectively, i.e. has there been 'value for money' (cost-effectiveness) and does the degree of improvement warrant the expenditure of funds, staffing, time, energy and good-will?

On this last point, it is possible to be efficient without being effective; a teacher may teach very well and achieve good test or examination results with limited resources, but may follow a scheme which does not match the needs of the pupils or the objectives of the school. It is also possible to be effective without being efficient; a teacher may achieve good test or examination results in a relevant subject but may do so only at great cost, perhaps at the expense of other parts of the curriculum or work of the team, department or subject.

The evaluation (and OFSTED inspection) of efficiency is largely a summative exercise which draws upon all evidence relating to:

- the provision, accessibility and use of resources which include finance, time, staff and the learning and teaching resources;
- the quality of management, planning and decision making (including financial decisions);
- the extent to which these contribute to the raising of standards of achievement and the development of the pupils in the school.

It is in considering the above points that decisions about the initiative undertaken can be made. Where there is serious shortfall at evaluation there needs to be a review process to identify the reasons for the 'failure' (or indeed the success). This is the review process, a type of post-mortem, on each of the stages of the planning process as shown in Figure 2 (p. 14), to identify the possible causes of the failure or success. Where there is identified failure at a particular stage (e.g. too ambitious or wrong time scale), the review process should enable the team to recover and overcome the difficulty rather than simply accepting failure. Of equal importance is the review where the process has been successful, i.e. can this successful approach be replicated in subsequent planning activities?

The review process should also be used on those plans and policies that are apparently operating successfully. This will ensure that the systems are up to date and in line with any changes in school, LEA or government policies. A good example of this is the statutory requirements for assessment, recording and reporting which have changed fairly frequently. Here there is simply a need to ensure that the team/department policy is modified in line with any amendments made at national level.

ESTABLISHING A TEAM VISION

A good vision will:

- be based on an analysis of the existing state of the team/department;
- be in agreement with the wishes and preferences of the team/department;
- consider all available options;
- include the motivating forces that will ensure progress;
- be realistic and achievable in the long term.

The key outcomes of subject leadership, given in *Supplement KE3*, form the basis for a team vision and the outcomes of the following exercises might well be compared with this national vision.

There are several training exercises which can be used to enable a team to investigate the establishment of a vision. The meaning of a team vision was explored in Part 1 and this should be clarified first so that members have some understanding of the concept of vision. Establishing a vision involves identifying it, sharing it, agreeing it and, perhaps the most difficult part, keeping it central to all of the future work of the school, department or team.

One method that has been used is to ask each member to draw a picture of his/her vision of the school/department/team. This should be done on a piece of A3 or flip chart paper and no words are to be used. The head or team leader then displays his/her drawing and explains the meanings within the drawing. Others, individually or in groups, then share their own examples. Once the worry of 'not being able to draw' is overcome, this approach can be quite revealing in indicating the positive and negative aspects which members show. An extension of the exercise is to ask groups or individuals to emphasise the positive elements of their 'vision' and to make suggestions as to how the negative aspects might be attacked and overcome.

A more common method of approaching the identification, sharing and agreement of the vision is for members, working individually, to answer questions or to complete sentences such as:

- What is the school's overall vision?
- Is this the obvious starting point for the establishment of a team vision?
- What are the best things about the school which must be fostered?
- What aspects of the work of our team are most successful/best done?
- What aspects does the team/department do badly at present?
- How is the team/department viewed by:

  - other teams/departments?
  - the school management team?
  - the governors?
  - the LEA?
  - the close clients, e.g. pupils and parents?

- From whom or what can the team/department learn?
- What should the team/department improve and how?
- What part should individuals play and how might this affect their roles?

- When should the team/department review its progress?
- If I were a parent considering sending my child to the school I should want. . . .
- If I were a pupil at the school I should want. . . .
- If I were a pupil choosing options I should choose (subject) because. . . .
- If I were head of the school I should want. . . .
- If I were a middle manager I should. . . .
- As a member of the support staff I should want. . . .
- As a teacher I should want. . . .
- In five years' time the school should be. . . .
- In five years' time the department/team should be or be seen as. . . .
- In five years' time the department/team will not. . . .

After 15–20 minutes of personal reflection and response, individuals or groups are asked to share and combine their views to produce a collective vision of the future.

These types of exercises are used as preparation stages in the establishment of the 'vision' and it is important, if progress is to be made, that consensus is achieved. However, it is unlikely that there will be a consensus view on all aspects at this first stage, particularly if the group is large. Thus, it is better to go ahead on areas of consensus even if some areas, where there is no consensus or there is strong disagreement, are omitted at the initial stage.

The point of these exercises is to give members an understanding of the concept of a 'vision' and to help in the acceptance of the need for this vision as an over-arching concept for the work of the team or department.

(Adapted from Bowring-Carr and West-Burnham 1994)

EXAMPLES OF AUDIT/MONITORING CHECKLISTS

Individuals in a team, or the whole team working towards the same end, work better if they have pointers or indicators in the form of checklists to ensure that all important issues are covered and nothing of importance is missed out. OFSTED inspection teams use such lists in their work in school inspections. Externally imposed checklists, however, are of less value than those generated by the groups or teams who are going to use them. The lists must be team and/or school specific and closely related to the overall intentions (the vision) of the team and the school.

In the same way, it would be inappropriate for the checklists to be imposed on the teams within the school (or individuals within a team) without first giving the teams (or individuals) a chance to develop ownership through a sharing and agreeing process in the formulation of the checklists.

As with the lists of performance indicators given in *Supplement P5*, the following are suggested issues which should be considered when carrying out reviews, monitoring or auditing of existing systems or when establishing new policies. They are designed to help in evaluating outcomes but are not exhaustive and should be adapted to the particular needs of the team and the context of the task being undertaken. Wherever appropriate and possible, the checklists should be quantified to facilitate comparative analysis. The lists will become a part of the quality assurance mechanism for the team and/or the school.

Policies and Planning

- How close is the team's vision to that of the school as a whole?
- How central is the team's vision to the planning and policy-making processes used?
- How clearly defined is the planning and policy-making process in terms of:

  - involvement and consultation?
  - the planning timetable?
  - 'publication' and dissemination?

- How systematic and objective are the monitoring procedures and the evaluation processes in order to inform future planning?
- How appropriate and effective is the information provided to guide planning and policy-making?
- What procedures are in place to ensure that team policies and plans are consistent with school intentions?
- Do those involved in policy-making and planning have the appropriate knowledge, skills and attributes?
- Is sufficient time given for planning, monitoring, evaluation and policy-making?
- Is all documentation organised logically and presented and written in clear and unambiguous language?

Curriculum

- To what extent is the curriculum co-ordinated and controlled to ensure that it provides for all pupils:

- breadth and balance?
- continuity and progression?
- relevance?
- equal opportunities (ability, gender and ethnicity)?

- Who is responsible for ensuring that the statutory requirements are met?
- To what extent does the curriculum allow differentiation of task as well as outcome?
- Do the schemes of work satisfy the needs of the least able and provide opportunities for the most able to be extended?
- How is the curriculum modified to account for those pupils with learning difficulties and linguistic needs?
- What processes are used for developing the curriculum?
- How are the schemes of work monitored and evaluated?

Teaching and Learning

- How does the team monitor and evaluate teaching and learning strategies to identify the most effective?
- What learning styles are most often displayed by the pupils?
- What is the balance between individual work, group work and whole class activities?
- To what extent does the work in class have elements of practical, reflective, conceptual and abstract/concrete, imaginative and creative activities?
- Are the pupils in any way involved when considering these processes?
- How does the team ensure continuous improvement in teaching and learning?

Oracy and Literacy (Communication Skills)

- What is the balance in lessons between speaking, listening, reading and writing?
- How does the team monitor each pupil's participation in these aspects?
- How does the team help pupils to analyse their strengths and areas in need of development?
- What range of reading materials is easily available to the pupils?
- How often does each pupil talk to the teacher about his/her reading?
- How does the team assess and recommend new books?
- What suitable reading materials are there in class, subject, department and school libraries?
- What use is made of electronically stored reading materials?
- What range of types/styles of writing are demanded of the pupils?
- What opportunities are given to each pupil to draft and redraft those pieces of writing which are considered important as learning outcomes?
- What is the range of readership addressed by the pupils?
- What use is made of information and communications technology in the pupils' literacy learning?
- When the questions above have been considered, is the team sure that, in the area of literacy and oracy, the ideals embodied in the school's aims/mission have been fulfilled?

Numeracy

- What opportunities are provided for number work across the curriculum?
- Are there other opportunities which could enhance the pupils' numerical skills?
- What other aspects of mathematics, e.g. graphical work, form a part of the curriculum?
- To what extent is the content of any mathematical work in other subjects co-ordinated with that of the mathematics scheme or mathematics department?
- Is the methodology used in mathematical aspects of the subject consistent with that recommended and used in the mathematics scheme of work?
- Does the use of mathematical aids, e.g. calculators (of all types), concur with the mathematics policy?
- To what extent is practical and investigative work included in the mathematics used?

Information and Communications Technology

- How much time is spent by each pupil using any item of ICT for curricular purposes?
- Does the team regard this time as sufficient?
- What are the constraints on the use of ICT by the pupils and how might these be lessened?
- Do the pupils regard ICT as a natural part of their work in the subject?
- What aspects of ICT predominate in the work of the pupils?
- Which aspects are in need of development for the teaching of the subject?
- What is the balance of individual and group work in ICT?
- To what extent do the teachers feel that they have the expertise in the use of ICT and what plans are in place for training to enhance the team's confidence?

Cross-curricular and Interdisciplinary Issues

- To what extent do the schemes of work contribute to the cross-curricular themes of:

  - economic and industrial understanding?
  - careers education and guidance?
  - health education?
  - education for citizenship?
  - the teaching of democracy?
  - environmental education?

- In what ways can the schemes be extended without adversely affecting existing content or methodology?
- In addition to the literacy, numeracy and ICT skills mentioned above, to what extent does the teaching and learning include the skills involved in:

  - problem solving?
  - personal and social aspects?
  - learning to learn (study skills)?

- To what extent do the schemes of work include reference to:
  - equal opportunities issues?
  - drug education?
  - sex education?
  - political education?
- Are these areas in line with school policies on the issues?

Staff Management

- Is the involvement of the department/team in staff selection procedures equitable and appropriate?
- Are the induction processes sufficiently informative and supportive?
- How are job descriptions developed, negotiated and used?
- Do the descriptions refer to what has to be done, not how it should be done? What is done to ensure equitable delegation of tasks, responsibilities and authority?
- What is done to minimise hierarchical and power-based relationships?
- What systems of support exist?
- How are training needs identified, prioritised and implemented?
- How much time do team leaders devote to 'coaching', counselling and mentoring members of the team?
- What is done to minimise bureaucracy, within the constraints of statutory requirements?

Resources

- How far are the spending plans an expression of the department/team vision and development plan?
- How does the team ensure that all resource decisions are focused on pupil learning?
- To what extent are staff teaching programmes and the timetable expressions of the individual learning and development needs of pupils (and teachers)?
- To what extent are the learning resources focused on the needs of the pupils?
- How do the processes of procurement ensure best value for money?
- What stock controls are in place?
- How are supplies maintained at an appropriate level without excesses?
- Is maximum use made of ICT to simplify management and administrative procedures?

Curriculum and Assessment

AUDIT OF CURRICULUM AND ASSESSMENT

The following is an example of how teams/departments might assess needs in relation to developing new, or reviewing existing, policies, documentation and procedures. The lists on pp. 124–7 cover the most important issues but are not necessarily comprehensive. There are elements which are applicable in only some phases/key stages. The lists may need customising.

This supplement, or a modified form of it, may be used collectively, with all members contributing, or be completed by individuals followed by a sharing of the outcomes. The latter approach should indicate the level of common understanding and awareness of the work of the team/department, in this case on curriculum and assessment. Completion of this type of supplement may also identify training needs for some or all of the team/department.

The columns in the lists indicate:

Key	
1	Implemented and working effectively
2	In place but in need of review; not a priority at present
3	Needs to be done or reviewed; priority indicated by a, b, c, etc.

Curriulum:	1	2	3
• complies with the 1988 Education Reform Act:			
– Common Requirements and General Requirements, if appropriate			
– in line with the recent changes in Key Stages 1 to 3			
– adaptable to take on changes in Key Stage 4 and Post-16			
• fulfils the requirements for the teaching of literacy and numeracy as well as information and communications technology			
• fulfils any OFSTED comments for action			
• documentation including:			
– department/subject curriculum policy			
– curriculum guidelines – for school brochure, options booklets, parents, etc.			
– schemes of work for all year groups/sets			
– lesson plans			
• pupils' perceptions of the curriculum experiences			

Statutory requirements to teach the National Curriculum:	I	2	3
• Extent to which the curriculum and organisation contribute to:			
– continuity and progression			
– pupils' attainment			
– pupils' responses			
– teachers' experience and expertise			
• opportunities for pupils to cover required elements in appropriate depth:			
– match of programmes of study and attainment targets to classroom practice			
– time allocation to curriculum components			
– differentiation strategies			
– literacy and numeracy timetabled in primary schools			

Equality of opportunity and access for all pupils:	I	2	3
• Curriculum planning and implementation (differentiation) take account of:			
– age			
– ability			
– learning styles and teaching methodologies			
– learning needs including prior learning experience			
– gender			
– ethnicity			
– special educational needs including linguistic needs			
– teaching group organisation			
• access for all pupils to National Curriculum Programmes of Study			
– Individual Education Programmes			
– disapplications			
• time allocations according to pupil needs and aspirations			
• accessibility of post-16 provision			

Curricular provision for pupils with Special Educational Needs:	1	2	3
• liaison with SEN department/SENCO			
• record of specific learning needs			
• learning objectives defined through IEPs where appropriate			
• any disapplications			

Continuity and progression in curricular planning:	1	2	3
• between years and across the Key Stages			
• inclusion of aspects of numeracy, literacy and ICT capability			
• cross-curricular links with other departments			
• liaison with other establishments, particularly primary/middle and post-16 provision			

Assessment of pupils' attainment:	1	2	3
• assessment arrangements in place for tests and teachers' assessments including:			
– observations of practical and oral work			
– written work completed in class			
– homework			
– results of school examinations and tests			
• common departmental marking policy, in line with school policy			
• opportunities for pupil self-assessment			
• procedures for determining test and examination entry levels, including pupil and parent liaison/consultation			

Recording of achievement data on pupils:	I	2	3
• data on prior attainment available (benchmarking)			
• system for storing and retrieval of the initial and subsequent attainment data on pupils			
• target setting by teachers			
• target setting by pupils			
• departmental system for easy access to, and transfer of, assessment records for individual pupils			
• use of value added approaches to compare with other departments and for year on year department/subject comparisons			

Reporting on pupils:	I	2	3
• procedures for the statutory reporting on:			
– Key Stage I pupils			
– Key Stage 2 pupils			
– Key Stage 3 pupils			
– Key Stage 4 and beyond			
– school leavers			
– pupils moving schools			
– pupils with statements			
• contributions to the National Record of Achievement			
• liaison with and feedback from parents			
• parents' evenings procedures			

SCHEMES OF WORK

Effective curriculum planning leading to schemes of work, to be used as working documents, is an important starting point for improving the quality of teaching and learning and thereby raising pupils' achievement.

In schools surveyed and reported on recently by OFSTED (1998), there was always someone with the responsibility for drawing up the scheme of work. However, the quality of the schemes of work in different subjects varied across and within schools. Consistently good practice in approaches to curriculum planning across a range of subjects was achieved in relatively few schools. The following is an example of good practice where the school management team gave firm guidance about the structure and detail to be included:

> The guidelines for the schemes of work give all heads of department a framework which ensures that they undertake detailed curriculum planning and give clear guidance on how subjects are to be taught. All schemes of work in this school list appropriate programmes and give helpful guidance on teaching and learning practices, as well as policies for marking and assessment. The schemes have proved extremely helpful, not only to members of the team involved in their production but also to teachers new to the school, part-time and supply teachers as well as students involved in initial teacher training. Newly appointed heads of department are introduced carefully to the guidelines to ensure that consistency of practice is maintained.

The outcome of effective curriculum planning is a scheme of work which underpins the whole work of the department/year group or in the subject, brings consistency to the teaching and helps to secure high standards. In the most effective teams or departments, the scheme is subject to continuous monitoring and review so that it always reflects best practice. Such monitoring may often be fairly informal but needs to be supplemented with more formal monitoring and evaluating procedures, including classroom observation, if it is to be fully effective at the implementation stage.

Key questions for the evaluation of schemes of work are:

- Does the scheme of work provide a long-term plan, in outline, to show how the curriculum is to be covered over the term, year or key stage?
- Are there more detailed short- and medium-term plans, e.g. half-termly, which provide a week-by-week breakdown of what is to be taught?
- Are there periods or lessons for revision and reinforcement?
- Does the scheme of work show specific learning outcomes and assessment opportunities for each unit of work?
- Are suggested teaching approaches, learning activities and key resources listed?
- Is differentiation included to account for the range of ability of the pupils?
- Does the scheme of work link directly to records of pupil progress and IEPs where appropriate?
- Is there space on the scheme to allow teachers to make comments on the effectiveness of the programme in the classroom (an example of the monitoring and formative evaluation processes in the implementation phase)?
- Does the school, department, subject or key stage team have an agreed format which supports continuity and progression within and across year groups and key stages?
- Does the scheme indicate at what stage there will be a review session for summative evaluation and possible revision?

BENCHMARKING AND TARGET SETTING

Benchmarking

Since 1 September 1998, schools have been required to set targets in relation to the performance of pupils in National Curriculum assessments and public examinations. In order to support the target-setting process, schools were provided with information about the performance of schools with similar characteristics to their own (benchmark information) against which they are able to compare their performance.

Schools have traditionally identified some benchmarks for pupils on entry but these benchmarks were often restricted to personal, social, health and behavioural information. Collecting prior attainment data was always more difficult because of a lack of consistent or standardised measures of pupil achievement from the number and variety of feeder schools, although most schools made attempts to identify those pupils with special educational needs. Most schools administer some form of screening (including pre-school screening information) or testing early in the year of entry but the reliability of these measures at such an early stage after entry has to be carefully analysed and re-checked once the pupils have 'settled' into their new environment.

The introduction of National Curriculum assessment at the end of Key Stages is now providing much more consistent data, giving more reliable baseline measures of attainment. Schools should use these baseline measures to monitor the progress of individual pupils as they move through to Key Stages and to public examinations at 16+ and 18+. This process will, of course, be easier in the core subjects of English, mathematics and science but these assessments may also give some overall measure of the level of pupil attainment which can be used in other areas of the curriculum. In addition, the statutory requirement and more uniform approach to reporting to receiving schools will also provide much valuable information for baseline assessments in all areas of the curriculum as well as other aspects of pupils' progress.

It is of great importance, therefore, that all teams or departments collect information at individual pupil level which will give an indication of a baseline measure which can be used for target setting as well as providing opportunities to monitor the progress of individual pupils and groups as they move through the school.

In addition to this, the QCA sends national benchmarking information to all schools in the Autumn term each year. This should provide valuable contextual information for the setting of targets by all schools. Some LEAs also provide similar local information from all of their maintained schools and some of the data supplied will be of a 'value added' type which makes the comparative use of the data much more significant (see *Supplements CA4* and *CA5*).

The first of the national benchmarking information was provided by the QCA in 1998. This was based on the 1997 national data for Key Stage 3 (test results and teacher assessments) and Key Stage 4 (GCSE results) in relation to the percentage of pupils, in the whole school, who were eligible for free school meals. Additional information was also provided on the GCSE performance of pupils in selective and secondary modern schools. This gave some indication of performance in relation to prior attainment and it is the intention to build on the information in subsequent years, although it is expected that LEAs will also use the national data to begin or extend work on local analyses.

Target Setting

The DfEE and OFSTED defined target setting as:

> Taking action by setting specific goals and targets designed to raise educational standards.
>
> (*Improving Schools*, 1994)

The link between the raising of standards and target setting is for many schools a new, complex and slow process. In addition, there is no universally accepted approach; schools, departments or individual teachers must find their own strategies to attack the problem. However, one common characteristic of effective target setting in schools is the generation of higher expectations which teachers have of pupils and which pupils have of themselves.

Surveys of schools have identified the following main characteristics associated with effective target setting, which can be equally applied at Key Stage/departmental/subject level as well as individual teacher/pupil level:

- Best practice stems from critical reflection and analysis of performance at school and all other levels;
- Best results obtain where departments, teams, teachers and pupils are fully involved in the process of establishing their own targets rather than targets being imposed without going through this process;
- In addition to monitoring and review of past performance, there is use of past and current data to focus effort and resources on pupils who are underachieving or being insufficiently challenged;
- When there is effective target setting, teams/departments can more easily show what is being aimed for by pupils;
- Target setting is successful when it is carefully and precisely planned so that each teacher can take responsibility for the setting and achieving of targets;
- The strategies adopted for improvement often place greater emphasis on pupils doing better rather than teachers being more effective;
- Improvement in pupil attainment is dependent on a range of factors, including the culture and leadership of the team or department, as well as the strategies adopted;
- Information from LEAs, as well as national data, can help schools and departments to:
  - evaluate their performance;
  - compare themselves on a year by year basis;
  - compare themselves with similar schools and departments;
  - set demanding but realistic, short-term targets.

The DfEE has identified effective use of target setting with the acronym SMART, viz. Specific, Measurable, Achievable, Realistic, and Time-related. Examples of the first two of these are pupils' performances in tests and examinations, and attendance rates. The other three aspects have to be related to the context of the school, key stage or department and its phase of development in the process of benchmarking and target setting.

When setting targets, schools will also need to take into account national targets which will be set from time to time. For example, the government has set national targets for:

- 11 year-olds:

  80 per cent (65 per cent) reaching the expected standard for their age in literacy;
  75 per cent (59 per cent) reaching the standard in numeracy;

- 16 year-olds:

  50 per cent (46.3 per cent) achieving 5 or more GCSEs at Grades A*–C;
  95 per cent (93.4 per cent) achieving 1 or more GCSEs at Grades A*–G;

- 19–21 year-olds:

  85 per cent (73.9 per cent) of 19 year-olds with a NVQ level 2 qualification;
  60 per cent (52.1 per cent) of 21 years-olds with a NVQ level 3 qualification;

- adults:

  50 per cent (45.0 per cent) with a NVQ level 3 qualification;
  28 per cent (26.0 per cent) with a NVQ level 4 qualification;

- organisations:

  45 per cent (19 per cent) of large- or medium-sized organisations recognised as Investors in People;
  10,000 (2,334) small organisations recognised as Investors in People.

The figures in brackets indicate the targets reached in 1998. Further national targets are in the process of consideration and consultation.

Target setting does not, of course, necessarily lead to a raising of standards and an improvement in pupils' achievements. However, it is a process, as a part of any development planning, that will clarify and provide a focus for such planning, i.e. it establishes success criteria.

The introduction of national performance tables has led many schools to institute a 'targeting' procedure, as opposed to target setting, for specific pupils or groups of pupils (e.g. at 16+ to target pupils who were judged to be at the Grade D/C borderline for GCSE). This is clearly an attempt to increase the proportion of pupils gaining the 'higher grades' in the national performance tables. Whilst this may be laudable, there has been a tendency in some schools to focus attention on only some pupils in any year group to the possible detriment of other pupils, particularly those who were unlikely to gain at least Grade D or indeed those who were certain to gain Grades A*–C. The process of target setting, and indeed targeting, should be applied to all pupils irrespective of their anticipated performance.
(see *From Targets to Action*, DfEE 1997, and *1997 Benchmark Information for Key Stages 1 and 2 and 3 and 4*, QCA 1998)

VALUE ADDED APPROACHES AT SUBJECT/ DEPARTMENTAL/YEAR GROUP LEVEL
(*see also Supplement CA5*)

In 1994 the SCAA (now QCA) described 'value added' as:

> Normal academic progression is the average progression that would be expected over a particular period, for pupils from a given starting point. The Value Added is the extent to which pupils may, over the same period, have exceeded or fallen below the expected progression from a given point.
>   (*Value Added Performance Indicators for Schools*)

The value added by a school is the overall contribution that the school makes to the total development of each of its pupils. Traditionally, when reporting to parents, this was simply described as 'pupil progress' but was often a vague, ill-defined comment and was open to a variety of interpretations.

Value added is the sum total of a pupil's development, from a baseline starting point. Many of these aspects of development are not easily measurable and therefore there is a tendency to work only on the aspects of development which can be quantified. It is dangerous, therefore, to believe that value added measures represent the 'Holy Grail' in terms of calculating the contribution of a school, department or subject to each pupil's overall development.

Value added measures simply make use of a more accurate gauge, than the raw results data, of the quantifiable aspects of pupil, departmental and school achievement, progress and development (improvement or decline). On examination performance, it is a way of measuring school or departmental performance/improvement which is more informative and useful than the raw data in simple percentages that is so often used (e.g. percentage Grades A–C, A–G, etc.).

The Dearing Report on the National Curriculum and assessment (SCAA 1994) made proposals for the introduction of some form of value added measure rather than using raw scores in examinations/tests in national performance tables. The working group suggested three possible models:

- Simple Linear Model – comparing academic performance with a measure of prior ability; there are difficulties at present for a national approach on this basis as Key Stage levels are not sufficiently discriminating, although it has been suggested that the levels for the core subjects could be aggregated for each pupil (i.e. 0–10 as a score for each pupil at Key Stages 1, 2 or 3);
- Estimating the proportions of pupils achieving results which are better or worse than expected – used at present by some schools to predict examination/test performance;
- Tri-partite Division – rather than the present 'league' tables, to divide schools into three groups, those achieving roughly as national data (within one standard deviation), those better than expected and those achieving less well (across the results for three years).

There are many examples already in use in LEAs of these three basic models which started with easily measured aspects of performance, e.g. A level performance compared with previous GCSE results and GCSE performance compared with previous level of academic measure.

These value added measures are not absolute (they have their limitations) but are better performance indicators than the simple percentages and averages used at present and therefore have greater value as a means of setting national targets for school improvement and of schools setting their own targets.

The 'simplest' model, and the one most often used in secondary schools, is performance at 16+ (GCSE) compared with some measure of attainment at intake (11+, 12+ or 13+). These two performance levels are plotted against each other for each pupil. In the example shown in Figure 4, individual pupil data on GCSE performance are plotted against a measure of prior ability, in this case the average of two Verbal Reasoning (VR) scores for each of the pupils. The GCSE results are quantified (using the scale Grade A* =8, Grade A = 7, Grade B = 6 , Grade C = 5, etc.) and the numbers are aggregated for each pupil, irrespective of how many subjects they entered. This is better than using an average score which would mean that the performance of a pupil gaining one Grade C was the same as a pupil gaining nine Grade Cs or another with nine Grade Cs and a Grade D. The plotting of the points for each pupil produces a scattergram and the 'line of best fit' (regression line) is then drawn on it as shown in Figure 4.

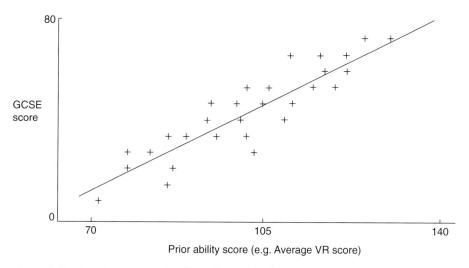

Figure 4 Pupil performance at GCSE against prior ability score

Pupils whose plotted points appear above the line of best fit have positive added value, i.e. they have performed better than predicted by the prior ability score, whereas those below the line have negative added value, i.e. they have performed less well than might have been predicted by their earlier performance.

The overall school, or department, performance is measured by the position and slope of the 'line of best fit' as is shown in Figure 4. Where there are data for LEA results from all schools an LEA line of best fit can be drawn. Then the performance of each school, i.e. the position and slope of the line of best fit for each school, can be compared with the LEA average. Similarly, it is possible to compare the performances of any of the schools in the Authority. Where there are no overall LEA data, use of this approach is limited to an individual school carrying out a year on year comparison which can be used to measure the improvement or otherwise over time.

It is also possible to use this approach to indicate the performance of pupils in any subject by comparing the GCSE score in the subject with the same pupils' overall GCSE performance, i.e. a departmental line compared with a school line. In the graph shown in Figure 5, the school line is drawn using the aggregated GCSE score (up to 80 in this case) for each pupil and the departmental lines (Lines A and B) are drawn using the subject GCSE score (up to 8, i.e. a Grade A*) for each pupil.

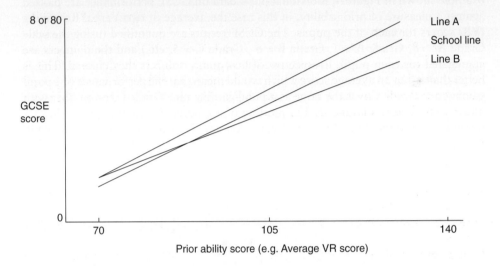

Figure 5 Subject performance against overall school performance

In this example, Line A shows that the subject/department has achieved better results across the full ability range, but particularly with the most able, than the school overall GCSE performance for the same pupils; Line B shows that the subject/department has performed better with the less able pupils but less well with the more able pupils. Using this general information the department can review its schemes of work and teaching strategies in an attempt to provide optimum chances of development for all pupils.

This approach could also be used to:

• act as a benchmarking tool for target setting for the following year for both the school and the departments;
• compare the results according to gender – separate lines for boys and girls;
• compare results for each subject and set;
• compare the performance of pupils entered for different tiers, examinations or Examination Boards in the same subject;
• investigate more thoroughly the pupils who have markedly over- or under-performed, at school or subject level, in order to identify possible causes and so be able to plan strategies to encourage or prevent, as appropriate, similar occurrences in future years.

Age differences within year groups was a significant, and unexpected, outcome in work done on value added measures by Shropshire LEA in the early 1990s (Jesson 1994). An analysis was done of overall GCSE performance (aggregate scores) against month of birth of the Year 11 cohort. There was a clear indication of differences, with pupils born in September performing better overall than pupils born in the following August. The only explanation given was a residual effect of the different starting points in formal schooling at the age of five!

In all value added analyses, the quality, reliability and validity of the data are important, particularly when small samples of pupils' results are being analysed. More expert statistical help (from the mathematicians/statisticians in the school or the LEA) may be required before attempting to draw other than the broadest of conclusions. However, it is still possible to measure the performance of departments where the numbers of pupils are small and the use of a 'value added line' is unreliable. As results are collected at individual pupil level, the quantified grade in the subject can be compared with the overall average quantified grade for each pupil. The difference between these two values will give a positive (better performance) or negative (poorer performance) value for each pupil. Once again this information can be used to set departmental targets for subsequent groups of pupils.

In order to use value added measures, reliable data on pupils must be collected at school and subject/department level. This might include:

- all Key Stage results, GCSE, A & AS Levels and GNVQ/NVQ (once an equivalence with GCE and GCSE is agreed); however, at school and departmental level, any reliable results/outcomes can be used to evaluate performance on a year by year basis;
- measures of ability of pupils on entry (but care needs to be taken with the reliability of results of any tests done early in the first term in a new school before the pupils have had time to settle, physically and emotionally, into their new environment);
- reading ages;
- dates of birth/age;
- results of any whole year group assessments (standardised);
- entry screening data.

Other, often more sensitive, data may be useful in the more detailed analyses of results at school, departmental, teaching group or individual pupil levels:

- free school meals data;
- social status data;
- single-parent families;
- number of siblings and pupil's position in the family;
- ethnicity;
- pupils from homes where English is not the first language;
- behaviour;
- pupil attitudes to school and subjects;
- number of schools previously attended;
- attendance/absence records;
- illnesses at critical times;
- other significant life events.

When using value added measures, questions to consider might include:

- Which benchmarks or prior ability measures should be used?
- How is it possible to quantify non-GCSE Performance (GNVQ/NVQ) and the less easily measured data, e.g. Free School Meals (although data are now being provided to LEAs by QCA)?
- When to begin – where such data are not yet available, collection should begin as soon as possible, since there is a long 'run-in' time for schools and departments even to begin year on year comparisons;
- Who co-ordinates and does the analyses at school and year group/departmental levels?
- Is expert statistical help available within the school or LEA?
- Is there an LEA programme in operation or an officer working on this aspect of performance for school improvement?*
- Has contact been made with the National Value Added Project – QCA – for reference to existing schemes?*
- Have existing projects and schemes been investigated?*

---

* Many LEAs have schemes for value added measures already in operation and the CEM Centre, University of Newcastle (see p. 204) has several projects covering value added schemes.

REPORTING ARRANGEMENTS

Much of the detail given below is the responsibility of the school (headteacher) rather than of the middle managers. However, the information is important to ensure that those responsible for teams and subjects are aware of the information they need to provide and keep at subject level in order that the school responsibility in complying with the reporting requirements can be met.

Although the general pattern is not likely to change, the detailed requirements may be varied, possibly year by year, and it is necessary to check the current regulations by referring to the latest QCA/DfEE booklet, *Assessment and Reporting Arrangements*, which is usually produced annually. This booklet also contains photocopiable proformas for reporting with completed examples, advice on good report writing and examples of the text of reports. In addition the booklet has the national performance data for the previous academic year.

A written report on children's achievements must be sent to their parents once during the school year. It is open to schools to issue more than one report, provided that the minimum information is sent to parents *by the end of the summer term*. The minimum requirements (as at 2000) are given below for each Key Stage.

Reception to Year 2

For children in their first term at school:

- Parents must be offered a reasonable opportunity to discuss the outcomes of baseline assessment with their child's teacher;
- This meeting should be within the term in which the baseline assessment has taken place; teachers may wish to consider making the results available to parents as a part of this discussion or, if a parent asks to see a copy of the results, the school should make this available.

For all children in Reception and above:

- Brief comments on the child's progress in each subject and activity studied as a part of the school curriculum; these should highlight strengths and development needs;
- The child's general progress;
- Arrangements for parents to discuss the report with a teacher at the school.

For all children of compulsory school age:

- The total number of sessions (half days) since the child's last report or since the child entered the school, whichever is later, and the percentage of sessions missed through unauthorised absence.

Additional information for children at the end of Key Stage 1:

- The child's National Curriculum assessment levels:
  - a statement that the levels have been arrived at by statutory assessment; schools may wish to differentiate between grades C–A at level 2, with level 2B and above

being regarded as the nationally expected level of achievement for most children at the end of Key Stage 1;
  – a statement where any attainment target has been disapplied;
  – a brief commentary setting out what the results show about the child's progress in the subject individually, and in relation to other children in the same year, drawing attention to any particular strengths and weaknesses;

• The percentage of children at the school at each level of attainment at the end of Key Stage 1;
• The previous year's national percentage of children at each level of attainment at the end of Key Stage 1.

Where the child is in the final year of a Key Stage 1, a parent may ask about the child's levels in each attainment target of any subject where statutory assessment has taken place. If the parent has not already been given this information, it must be provided within 15 school days of the request.

Transfer from Key Stage 1 to 2

Where there is a transfer to a new school at the end of Key Stage 1, teachers from both schools might usefully agree the most appropriate timing for the transfer of assessment information. For teacher assessments this would best be done before the end of the term preceding the transfer. Funding is available, under the Standards Fund; School Improvement Grant to support the transfer arrangements (contact QCA Key Stage 1 Team; see p. 200).

Key Stage 2: Years 3–6

Where information, such as the results of National Curriculum assessments, is not available before the end of the summer term, schools must ensure that it is sent to parents as soon as practicable, and in any case no later than 30 September.
For all children in Years 3–6:

• Brief comments on the child's progress in each subject and activity studied as a part of the school curriculum; these should highlight strengths and development needs;
• The child's general progress;
• Arrangements for parents to discuss the report with a teacher at the school;
• The total number of sessions (half days) since the child's last report or since the child entered the school, whichever is later, and the percentage of sessions missed through unauthorised absence.

Additional information for pupils at the end of Key Stage 2:

• The child's National Curriculum assessment levels

  – a statement that the levels have been arrived at by statutory assessment;
  – a statement where any attainment target has been disapplied;
  – a brief commentary setting out what the results show about the child's progress in the subject individually, and in relation to other children in the same year, drawing attention to any particular strengths and weaknesses;

- The percentage of pupils at the school at each level of attainment at the end of Key Stage 2;
- The previous year's national percentage of pupils at each level of attainment at the end of Key Stage 2.

Where the child is in the final year of Key Stage 2, a parent may ask about the child's levels in each attainment target of any subject where statutory assessment has taken place. If the parent has not already been given this information, it must be provided within 15 school days of the request.

Transfer from Key Stage 2 to 3

Recent research by Homerton College (DfEE 1999) concluded that schools need to focus more specifically on expectations of teaching and learning in Key Stage 3. Identified good practice included:

- Year 6 and 7 teachers working in each other's classrooms;
- Bridging units, such as those developed by QCA, which start in Year 6 and are completed in Year 7;
- Target setting between pupil and teacher at the start of Year 7.

Where pupils transfer to a new school at the end of Year 6, teachers from both schools might usefully agree the most appropriate timing for the transfer of assessment information. For teacher assessments this would best be done before the end of the term preceding the transfer. Funding is available, under the Standards Fund; School Improvement Grant to support the transfer arrangements.

Key Stage 3: Years 7–9

Where information, such as results of National Curriculum assessments, is not available before the end of the summer term, schools must ensure that it is sent to parents as soon as practicable, and in any case no later than 30 September.
For all pupils in Years 7–9:

- Brief comments on the pupil's progress in each subject and activity studied as a part of the school curriculum; these should highlight strengths and development needs;
- The pupil's general progress;
- Arrangements for parents to discuss the report with a teacher at the school;
- The total number of sessions (half days) since the pupil's last report or since the pupil entered the school, whichever is later, and the percentage of sessions missed through unauthorised absence.

Additional information for pupils at the end of Key Stage 3:

- The pupil's National Curriculum assessment levels:

  - a statement that the levels have been arrived at by statutory assessment;
  - a statement where any attainment target has been disapplied;

- a brief commentary setting out what the results show about the pupil's progress in the subject individually, and in relation to other pupils in the same year, drawing attention to any particular strengths and weaknesses;

- The percentage of pupils at the school at each level of attainment at the end of Key Stage 3;
- The previous year's national percentage of pupils at each level of attainment at the end of Key Stage 3.

Where the pupil is in the final year of Key Stage 3, a parent may ask about the pupil's levels in each attainment target of any subject where statutory assessment has taken place. If the parent has not already been given this information, it must be provided within 15 school days of the request.

Transfer to Key Stage 4

Teachers might usefully use the period after the Key Stage 3 tests to:

- continue teaching aspects of the programme of study, often with activities which enrich pupils' understanding, provide opportunities for independent investigation or enable study in greater depth on specific aspects;
- provide feedback to pupils on their performance in the tests, including reference to the marked scripts when these are returned;
- introduce the outline of work to be done during Key Stage 4 (a summary scheme of work) and practise the necessary study skills that might be needed/used;
- work with pupils on target setting and action planning;
- provide wider experience, e.g. practical and field work, links with industry, residential events;
- provide induction for, or make an early start on, courses, e.g. GCSE, Part 1 GNVQ.

Key Stage 4 and Beyond: Years 10 and 11, and 12, 13 and 14+

Written reports must be sent at least once during the school year:

- to parents, where the pupil is aged under 18 years;
- to pupils, where they are 18 years or over.

Reports may be issued more than once a year provided the minimum requirements are met. Where information, such as the results of public examination results, is not available before the end of the summer term, schools must ensure that it is sent to parents as soon as practicable, and in any case no later than 30 September.
The requirements (which do not apply to school leavers – see p. 141) are as follows. For all pupils in Year 10 and all non-school leavers in Years 11–14+:

- Brief comments on the pupil's progress in each subject and activity studied as a part of the school curriculum; these should highlight strengths and development needs;
- The pupil's general progress;

- Arrangements for parents (or the pupil) to discuss the report with a teacher at the school;
- The subjects in which the pupil was entered for any GCSE and the grade achieved;
- Any other qualification or unit towards a qualification and the grade achieved (where available);
- The subjects in which the pupil was entered for any 'A' level or 'AS' examination and the grade achieved and the number of points scored, viz. Grades A–E = 10–2 points at 'A' level, and 5–1 points for 'AS'.

Comparative information about the attainments of pupils of the same age in the school and nationally is contained in the school performance tables for the area, the school prospectus and the governors' annual report, and must be available at the school for parents to look at on request.

For all pupils of compulsory school age in Years 10 and 11:

- Total number of sessions (half days) since the pupil's last report or since the pupil entered the school, whichever is the later, and the percentage missed through unauthorised absence.

Reports to School Leavers

Although the essential principles of reporting to parents remain the same, variations exist for reports on school achievements for pupils aged 16+, who are designated as 'leavers':

- the results of any public examinations, qualifications achieved and credits towards them, including vocational qualifications and their credits;
- brief particulars of achievements in other subjects and activities studied as a part of the school curriculum.

The National Record of Achievement must be used in the prescribed format when reporting on school leavers. It is essential to:

- include information about the examinations taken by the pupil, and qualifications, and credits towards qualifications, achieved on the form headed 'Qualifications and Credits';
- ensure that the form headed 'Qualifications and Credits' is signed by a teacher or tutor familiar with the pupil;
- include the 'brief particulars' of achievements in other subjects and activities studied as a part of the school curriculum in the final year on the form headed 'School Achievements';
- ensure that the form headed 'School Achievements' is signed and dated by a teacher who is familiar with the pupil and that there is provision for the pupil to sign the form.

For pupils aged 18 or over, the report must be directed to the pupil and provide the same information, but not necessarily in the same format.

Additional Reporting Information for all Key Stages

- Reports for the annual review of a child's/pupil's statement of SEN may, if schools wish, serve as the annual report to parents, but this must contain the minimum information required as above;
- In the absence of any court restrictions, divorced or separated parents who make themselves known to the school should be treated in the same way as the parent(s) with whom the pupil lives;
- National Curriculum and public examination results cannot be withheld by schools as a penalty for the non-return of school property; if necessary schools should seek redress through the small claims court;
- Headteachers may, if they wish, make available to parents a pupil's National Curriculum test scripts and, from 2000, examination boards' scripts;
- The length of time for which the school should retain these scripts is a matter for decision by the school;
- Schools issuing detailed reports on all National Curriculum subjects in the Spring term, when pupils are involved in option choices, need only report briefly at the end of Key Stage 3; the second report should concentrate on how pupils have performed in relation to the level descriptions or end of key stage descriptions;
- The school should decide whether or not to report pupils' attainment from teacher assessment by individual attainment targets, in addition to the statutory requirement to report teacher assessment by subject level or end of key stage description outcome.

Reports to Receiving Schools

For All Pupils

Headteachers must send to the pupil's new school (maintained or independent):

- a completed common transfer form (Ref. TF4);
- all educational records relating to the pupil (including the pupil's last annual report).

The common transfer form includes the following performance information:

- the pupil's Key Stage 3 statutory assessment results in the non-core subjects of design and technology, geography, history, IT and a modern foreign language by subject and, where available, by attainment target;
- brief statements of the pupil's attainment in relation to the end of Key Stage descriptions for art, music and physical education;
- the pupil's Key Stage 1 and 2 statutory assessment results (including those made by any previous school) in English, mathematics and science by subject and, where available, by attainment target;
- the results of any public examination (including those from any previous schools).

For Pupils of Compulsory School Age

The form must also include the teachers' latest assessments of the pupil's progress against attainment targets in the core and non-core subjects (as defined above) since the pupil's Key Stage 3 assessments or since the pupil arrived at the reporting school.

The Headteacher's Role in Reporting

It is important that those responsible for subjects, are aware of certain aspects of the powers and discretion that headteachers have on reporting which may be relevant to report writers. Headteachers may:

- exclude from reports to parents (or adult pupils) information which may breach a confidence, be harmful to the pupil or parents, or involve disclosing information about other pupils;
- decide, in the case of students aged 18 or over, whether to report attainments to their parents as well.

They have the power to exclude certain confidential information:

- which might identify someone else as a source of the information, or as the person to whom the information relates;
- which may cause serious harm to the pupil concerned or to any other person, e.g. in a case, or possible case, of child abuse;
- which would disclose the levels in any attainment target or subject of another pupil.

CROSS-CURRICULAR CONSIDERATIONS

Following the introduction of the National Curriculum in 1989, the National Curriculum Council published a pamphlet on the 'Whole Curriculum' (NCC 1992). This identified:

- the National Curriculum;
- the Basic Curriculum – the National Curriculum and Religious Education;
- the Whole Curriculum – the basic curriculum together with:

  - additional subjects beyond the National Curriculum;
  - cross-curricular elements;
  - extra-curricular activities.

Cross-curricular Elements

These were further considered under three headings: dimensions, themes and skills.

Dimensions

- These are concerned with the intentional promotion of pupils' personal and social development through the curriculum as a whole, not simply through separate courses of personal, social and health education;
- They need to be an explicit part of every school's curriculum policy;
- They should include all aspects of equal opportunities;
- They are the responsibility of all teachers and all schools.

Themes

- These extend pupils' knowledge and understanding, helping them to develop new concepts and skills;
- They involve questions of values and beliefs and encourage pupils to explore and develop their own feelings, values and attitudes;
- Examples are:

  - economic and industrial understanding;
  - careers education and guidance;
  - health education;
  - education for citizenship;
  - environmental education.

Skills

- These should be developed through the teaching in all subjects wherever and whenever possible and relevant;
- Examples are:

  - communication skills (oracy and literacy);
  - numeracy;

- study skills;
- problem solving;
- personal and social skills;
- information and communications technology.

Departments and curriculum co-ordinators have, of course, included many of the cross-curricular elements in their schemes of work and lesson planning, but it is perhaps not surprising that some of these elements have taken lower priority in the face of the implementation of the National Curriculum, its assessment arrangements and the subsequent revisions of both.

Significantly, however, both the previous and the present governments have emphasised three skills areas as priorities, viz. numeracy, literacy and information and communications technology, the first two of which are now given greater priority, in terms of time, in primary schools.

Interdisciplinary Aspects in the Curriculum

There are several areas of learning and development which schools provide within the curriculum that have implications for many of the other subject areas. These include the following:

Sex Education

The governors must have, and must keep up to date, a policy on sex education, a statement on which must appear in the school prospectus. Parents have the right to have their children wholly, or partly, excused from receiving sex education apart from those elements prescribed in the National Curriculum. As there is a statutory requirement to teach sex education, having due regard for moral considerations and the value of family life, it is likely that many teachers both in and out of the classroom will face this element of learning. The pastoral/guidance staff and the programmes they devise will need to be co-ordinated with other aspects of sex education taught in subject areas.

Drug Education

The statutory orders for the teaching of science will contain aspects of drug education in Key Stages 1 to 4. Once again, however, the 'tutorial' elements of the curriculum will also be considered when planning programmes. This is a difficult area which causes increasing concern in some schools.

Political Education

Schools and LEAs are statutorily obliged to prohibit:

- the pursuit of partisan political activities by any registered pupils who are junior pupils (presumably up to the age of 11);
- the promotion of partisan views in the teaching of any subject in the school.

When pupils are involved in extra-curricular activities where political issues are raised, they should be given a balanced experience of differing or opposing political views.

Careers Education

There will be a programme of careers education in all secondary schools and appropriate trained and experienced staff to deliver the programme. However, in recent years this area has taken on greater significance through government action. The DfEE publication *Better Choices* (1995) stated the aims of careers education and guidance:

- to prepare young people for adult and working life;
- to contribute to the development of the whole person;
- to foster the notion of responsible citizenship.

There is a tendency to consider careers education as an aspect that is introduced only towards the end of statutory schooling. While there is a need for greater emphasis from Year 9 onwards, the more specific references in *Better Choices* make it clear that some aspects of careers education should begin, in simple ways, in Key Stage 1. This should cover, as far as is relevant to younger pupils:

- knowledge of themselves and the choices and opportunities open to them;
- skills of decision making and managing change;
- positive attitudes of self-reliance and towards others.

Teaching and Learning

MONITORING AND EVALUATING THE QUALITY OF LEARNING AND TEACHING

All planning processes for change should consider all of the following issues:

- Why?   – everyone needs to be aware of, and to agree with, the reasons for the initiative;
- What?   – aims, intended outcomes and success criteria need to be agreed by all; consideration must be given to the ambition of the initiative;
- How?   – define the full process, including feedback process and the possible action on it;
- Who?   – within the team or across teams, who will do what and to whom?
- How much?   – effectiveness must be matched with time and cost;
- How often?   – what will be the timing of classroom observations?
- When?   – days and dates with start and end points;
- Training/Practice – of observers and observed, cf. the teacher appraisal (performance review?) and OFSTED criteria;
- Effect on pupils – do they need to be aware of the process?
- Monitoring   – including the process and method of feedback;
- Evaluation   – have the intended outcomes/targets been met?
- Feedback   – what form of feedback should be given to staff, pupils, SMT, governors?
- What next?   – follow-up action plans.

The criteria in Table 5 and the proformas in Tables 6 and 7 form a basis for the lesson observation process. Having considered the issues above and achieved a team consensus on the process, the criteria in Table 5, under each of the headings, should be the basis of any classroom observation. The list in Table 5 is comprehensive and it may be that the team or individuals decide on a particular number or range of the criteria, rather like the process described for the observation of a lesson in the case of newly qualified teachers described in Part 1. When using the proforma shown in Table 6, the grading of lessons is optional and it should not be allowed to become a major issue in observations, particularly in the early stages. Practice using the criteria is more important and gradings should be used only when all members are confident with the process of observation and all have a clear understanding of what the team means by the grades and what value these have within the team.

The proforma shown in Table 7 is a suggested approach to the feedback process between the observer and the teacher. Once again, the use of a proforma of this type needs practice and a sharing of experiences in a thoroughly open and professional way. The process should be positive but constructively critical and based on the assumption, and agreement, that all can improve.

Under the new staff review procedures, lesson observation and the criteria and feedback mechanism to be used may focus on particular aspects identified as areas for development for a teacher. The observations and the review meeting will therefore concentrate on these aspects and the observer should be aware of them before the observation.

Table 5 Criteria and guidance notes for classroom observation

Context	• group: age, ability, size • lesson context/activities/organisation/resources
Teaching: identify strengths and weaknesses and the impact on standards achieved by the pupils	• teacher sets clear learning objectives/intended outcomes • pupils know what, why, how, how long and standards expected • set in context of a well-planned overt scheme of work • teacher has secure command of subject/course and National Curriculum • match between activities and range of pupils' needs – differentiation • time and resources well used – appropriate time on task • questioning and feedback leads to new learning, clearer understanding and consolidation which challenges thinking • pupils are well managed, ensuring a high standard of discipline • praise used as often as appropriate • evidence of support for less able and challenge to more able • equal opportunities issues addressed • opportunities for pupils to develop independent learning skills • organisation allows positive and economic pupil:teacher interaction (e.g. room layout, individual, paired, small group, whole class activities) • pupils' work assessed, within class where possible, thoroughly, constructively and diagnostically • homework reinforces and/or extends learning • marking provides constructive and developmental feedback
Response: the degree to which the pupils learn effectively	• interest, motivation and perseverance in completing the task(s) • work collaboratively and independently as required and as appropriate • show respect for each other and for others' ideas, beliefs and values • show initiative and work independently • develop a capacity for personal study and endeavour • able to set targets • able to evaluate and improve their work
Attainment: what level have the pupils achieved?	• in relation to national norms • complemented by secure evidence of what pupils know, understand and can do (in their work in the lesson) • evidence of competence in speaking, listening, reading, writing and in numeracy and information and communications technology capability
Progress: measure of the rate of learning	• what have pupils gained from the lesson? • what do their work and their responses say about what they have learned and consolidated? • how does this progress compare with what should be expected for pupils at this level and how does it compare with other groups in the same year? • SEN pupils against their Individual Education Programmes and extension of the most able pupils
Other significant factors or evidence	• timetable: day/week, time for lesson • in-class support and other resources available • accommodation

Source: Handbook for the Inspection of Schools (OFSTED 1994).

Table 6 Lesson observation proforma

Teacher:	Observer:	Date/Period:
Form/Group:	Subject/Topic:	NOR/No. Present
Ability range:		Boys: / Girls: / Total: /

Context of lesson:

Evidence and evaluation

Teaching: ☐

Response: ☐

Attainment: ☐

Progress: ☐

Other significant factors or evidence:

Grading (optional): 0 = insufficient evidence; 1 = excellent; 2 = very good; 3 = good; 4 = satisfactory; 5 = unsatisfactory; 6 = poor; 7 = very poor.

Source: Handbook for the Inspection of Schools (OFSTED 1994).

Table 7 Lesson observation summary evaluation proforma

Teacher:	Observer:	Date:

Quality of Teaching:

Quality of Learning:

Action points arising:

Proposed review date:	Signed: Teacher: Observer: Date:

The Lesson Observation Summary Evaluation Proforma (Table 7) should be completed by the observer after each lesson or series of lessons observed. It should be discussed and the comments shared and agreed with the teacher. The outcomes should form part of the process of target setting for the teacher to assign objectives for future development.

AGREED POINTS OF LEARNING

The following brief list of agreed points of learning was drawn up by a group of teachers and educational psychologists. It provides a constant and important reminder to teachers about the way all pupils learn and the need always to be conscious of their teaching strategies.

- In any learning situation, the capacity of the learners is an important factor especially as regards their age and ability;
- Motivation is an important factor in learning;
- Excessive motivation, such as anxiety or fear, may impede learning;
- Rewards are superior to punishment as motivating factors;
- Intrinsic motivation is superior to extrinsic motivation;
- Tolerance of failure may best be countered by providing a background of success;
- Individuals need practice in setting themselves realistic targets;
- The previous learning experience of an individual should be taken into account;
- Active participation by the learner is better than passive reception such as listening and viewing;
- Relevant materials and tasks are mastered more readily;
- There is no substitute for repetitive practice of skills such as the memorisation of unrelated facts;
- Information about good performance, as well as mistakes, aids learning;
- Transfer of learning to new tasks is better if the learners can discover the relationships for themselves;
- Spaced recalls are an advantage in the long-term retention of learning.

THE LEARNING STYLE INVENTORY

This inventory is designed to explore the way in which you learn and to give an insight into the range and variety of ways in which pupils might learn.

The Task

- Look at the four statements a to d in each row (1 to 9) and decide how they refer to you. Give four marks for the statement (a to d) which best fits you, three for the second, two for the third and one for the statement least appropriate to you.
  NB There are no right or wrong answers.

	a		b		c		d	
1	I like to get involved		I like to take my time before acting		I am particular about what I like		I like things to be useful	
2	I like to try things out		I like to analyse things and break them into parts		I am open to new experiences		I like to look at all sides of issues	
3	I like to watch		I like to follow my feelings		I like doing things		I like to think about things	
4	I accept people and situations the way they are		I like to be aware of what is around me		I like to evaluate		I like to take risks	
5	I have gut feelings and hunches		I have a lot of questions		I am logical		I am hard working and get things done	
6	I like concrete things, things I can see, feel, touch or smell		I like to be active		I like to observe		I like ideas and theories	
7	I prefer learning in the here and now		I like to consider issues and reflect about them		I tend to think about the future		I like to see the results of my work	
8	I have to try things out for myself		I rely on my own ideas		I rely on my own observations		I rely on my feelings	
9	I am quiet and reserved		I am energetic and enthusiastic		I tend to reason things out		I am responsible about things	

Source: Adapted from Kolb and McCarthy (1980).

- Use the grids below to summarise your findings. Fill in the numbers you have given alongside 1a to 9d and total your scores.

NB Fill in only the scores asked for. Some items are not included, as this prevents the possible 'patterning' of responses.

CE Concrete – Experience	RO Reflective – Observational	AC Abstract – Conceptualisation	AE Active – Experimentation
1a	1b	2b	2a
2c	2d	3d	3c
3b	3a	4c	6b
4a	6c	6d	7d
8d	8c	8b	8a
9b	9a	9c	9d
TOTAL	TOTAL	TOTAL	TOTAL

The Learning Kite

Plot the four totals on a copy of the graph shown in Figure 6, to produce your Learning Kite. An example of a completed kite (the author's) is shown in Figure 7.

Examine your own kite:

- What does it tell you about the way in which you learn and the likely effect of this on the way you teach?
- How do the shapes of the kites vary within the team/department?
- To what extent do they vary and does this reflect any differences in each member's contribution to the teaching across the team?
- What would you expect to be the range of kite shapes in any group of pupils that you teach?
- Is it possible to use this technique with any of the groups that you teach, in order to assess the range of learner types within the group?
- How could you modify your teaching methodology, or increase the range of your teaching strategies, to take account of the range of learner types in the groups that you teach?

The numbers in the four quadrants are related to the generalised descriptions of the four learner types given in Tables 8–11 in *Supplement TL4*. These descriptions, together with the proforma in Figure 8 (also *TL4*), provide opportunities to take the analysis further in an exercise on lesson planning based on the likely spread of learner types in any teaching group.

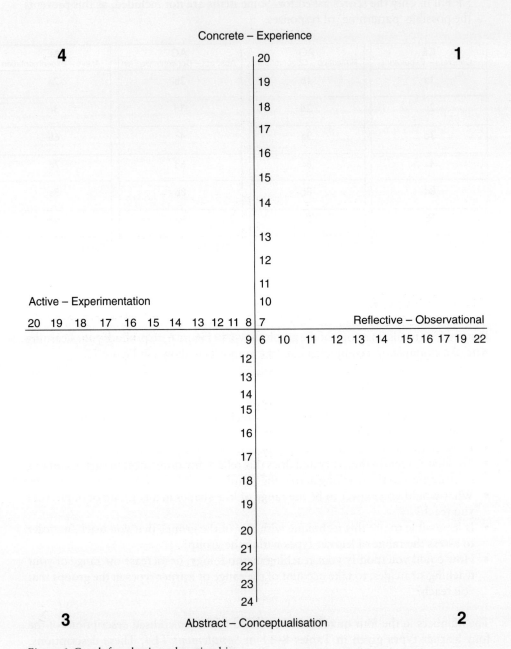

Figure 6 Graph for plotting a learning kite

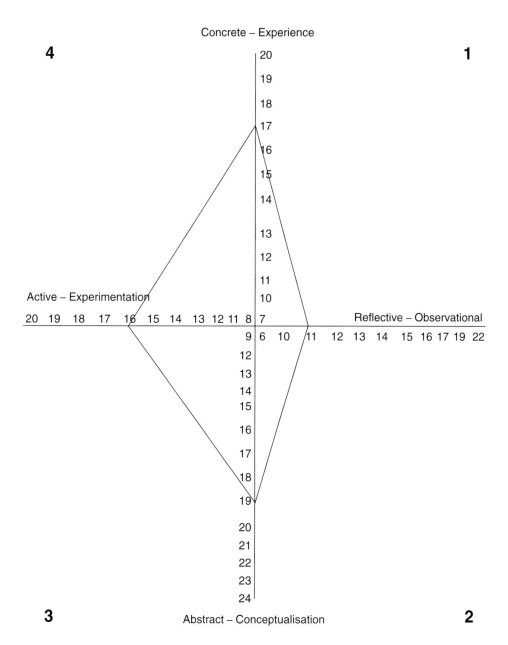

Figure 7 An example of a completed learning kite (the author's)

CHARACTERISTICS OF LEARNER TYPES AND LESSON PLANNING

Table 8 Generalised description of 'Type 1 Imaginative' learners

Advantages	Disadvantages
• see new ways of doing things • come up with creative solutions • see long-term implications of things • can see the total picture • unhurried, don't get in a flap • listen to others and share ideas • see connections between different subjects being studied • present work in novel and artistically appealing ways • good at coming up with new alternatives • pinpoint important new questions	• can't see the 'trees for the wood' – forget important details • wait too long before getting started • can be uncritical of ideas • don't organise work well • don't like work or revision timetables • only work with short bursts of energy • forget to bring key books etc. for homework • easily distracted from the job in hand • don't re-work notes or classify material • too easy going, not assertive enough with friends or teachers

Source: Kolb (1984).

Table 9 Generalised description of 'Type 2 Logical' learners

Advantages	Disadvantages
• organise facts and material well • see links between ideas • like to understand everything on the topic • curious, and enjoy problems • work things out well on paper • work well alone with minimum help from teachers and friends • precise and thorough • plan well in advance for essays, tests and exams • set clear goals, know why things are done, and what is of the highest priority • re-work essays and notes • good critics	• need too much information before getting down to work or allowing themselves an opinion • fail to use friends and teachers as resources • reluctant to try new approaches • can get bogged down in theory • like to do things in a set way – uncreative • don't trust feelings – their own or others' • don't function well in group discussions • keep problems to themselves • only trust logic • overcautious, don't like taking risks

Source: Kolb (1984).

Table 10 Generalised description of 'Type 3 Practical' learners

Advantages	Disadvantages
• work well on their own • are good at setting goals and making plans of action • know how to find information • see the applications of theories • get things done on time • don't get distracted • have revision timetables and work plans • organise time well and have time for other things • read instructions carefully • research test and examination papers thoroughly • have notes classified and filed	• are impatient with others' viewpoints • think there is only one way of doing something – their way! • fail to use friends and teachers as resources • 'can't see the wood for the trees' • get pre-occupied with details • lack imagination • poor at coming up with new questions • often don't work well with others • more concerned with getting the job done than with making sure it's really a good job • cut corners • not interested in presentation of their work

Source Kolb (1984).

Table 11 Generalised description of 'Type 4 Enthusiastic' learners

Advantages	Disadvantages
• get totally involved in something that interests them • work well with other people, ask for help, and talk through problems with others • enjoy writing freely – as it comes • will try any new idea or technique • generally like taking risks • work quickly and get others involved and enthusiastic too • like variety and excitement • are not concerned with making fools of themselves by asking questions or volunteering for something new • learn by talking with other people • skip reading books	• don't plan work in advance • rush into examination questions and essays without thinking them through • tend to neglect the subjects they are not interested in • not good at organising time • try to do too many things at once • not good at working out priorities • leave things to the last minute • can be demanding of friends • cannot be bothered with details • do not read through or check work • do not re-work notes or classify material

Source Kolb (1984).

Lesson Planning Assignment

Using the 'Kolb's approach', review or plan a lesson or topic of your choice in the quadrants below.

Lesson/Topic .... Yr Grp/Class ....

Ability Range ....

Objectives
(brief)..
....

Enthusuastic	Imaginative
Opportunities for: – open-ended experiments – pupil-initiated activity – pupil trial and error, etc.	Opportunities for: – imagination – divergent thinking – innovation, etc.
Practical	Logical
Opportunities for: – practising skills – doing structured practical work – showing practical applications, etc.	Opportunities for: – thinking logically – acquiring abstract info. – concept acquisition, etc.

Figure 8 Lesson review/plan, based on the approach of Kolb (1984)

The Task

- Write the various activities/phases of your chosen lesson in the appropriate quadrant in a copy of Figure 8. Review what you have written and, if the content and/or methodology in any one quadrant is weak, think of activities/methods of teaching which you could use to improve the plan.
- Share your plan with a colleague working with the same or a similar group of pupils.

Using Kolb's descriptions of learner types, all teachers could identify named pupils whom they have taught who would more or less fit one of these four descriptions. But, of course, all pupils will exhibit learning behaviours which fall into more than one of the categories. However, there is likely to be an emphasis on one of the four types with all pupils. In addition, pupils do not remain static in their learning styles. Many learn different approaches and indeed one of the reasons for teaching study skills, although not necessarily under this heading, is to broaden pupils' experience and expertise as learners. Similarly pupils will naturally develop as learners with age, experience, maturity and motivation. Teachers who have had experience of teaching adults will be very much aware of these changes.

The nature of subjects in the curriculum will of course have particular emphases on each of the four learner types. However, in the teaching of all subjects there is a need to ensure that all four areas are included in the teaching programmes. So often teachers teach according to the way in which they learned and, particularly in the early years of teaching, how they were taught. Teachers always need to be aware of the effects of their teaching style(s) on the learners.

There has been a great deal of research on both learning and teaching strategies and the government has recently commissioned further research into the characteristics of effective teaching in order to set a framework for teacher assessment and professional development.
In order to explore this difficult area of what constitutes effective teaching, teachers and teams should attempt to answer the following questions:

- In any group of learners being taught what is the range of learner types present?
- Is there a predominance of one type of learner in the group or class?
- If so, how has this been identified?
- What effect does this have on the teaching strategies used?
- As most groups will contain a mixture of learning styles, how does this affect the teaching approaches used?
- Are any pupils being disadvantaged because of the teaching approaches being used?
- How much is the teaching used a reflection of the teacher's learning style?
- How can you identify the need to modify the style?
- How can you attempt to modify your preferred style to match more closely all learners' needs?
- How can the teaching strategies used be modified to improve the learning of all pupils?
- How will you evaluate the effectiveness of any change of teaching style?

EFFECTIVE TEACHING SKILLS

Effective teachers show most (or all) of the following characteristics. They:

- have a high level of organisation, with thorough preparation and planning with clear objectives;
- create a climate in which learning takes place and manage the learning environment, ensuring the appropriate level of discipline;
- have high expectations of pupils and are able to interest, challenge and motivate them;
- are enthusiastic for, and have a thorough grasp of, their subject;
- plan lessons which are purposeful, appropriately paced and offer all pupils the opportunities to enhance their motivation and self-esteem;
- are able to introduce lessons through effective whole class questioning and to summarise the learning outcomes at the end of lessons;
- have an effective teaching style and delivery, with appropriate variety of strategies for whole class, group and individual work and are able to cope with the range of ability through appropriate differentiation of tasks;
- are able to manage the teaching time effectively in relation to the tasks set and the abilities of the pupils;
- provide opportunities for assessment, including pupil self-assessment where appropriate and relevant;
- ensure that pupils leave the lesson with new knowledge, understanding and/or skills;
- set relevant homework which supports and/or extends the classwork and which is accessible by all of the pupils;
- use accurate and thorough marking which gives informative feedback and helps the pupils to understand their strengths and areas in need of improvement and development;
- keep accurate and readily accessible records;
- evaluate the learning in, and teaching of, their lessons;
- work collaboratively and supportively with colleagues to improve learning in the subject;
- undertake regular and appropriate professional development.

EVALUATING LEARNING AND TEACHING: THE PERCEPTIONS OF THOSE INVOLVED

A method of monitoring or evaluating the effectiveness of learning and teaching is the use of questionnaires to test the perceptions of those involved. This is particularly helpful if a new approach, syllabus or scheme of work is about to be, or has just been, introduced. A questionnaire before and after the event should give an indication of the changes, and possibly the improvements, that have been perceived by the key stakeholders in the process.

The Pupils' Perceptions

The questions, language and methods (e.g. oral approaches with certain pupils) should be varied according to the ages and abilities of the pupils and it is important that all pupils have some understanding of why it is being done. However, whatever their age or ability, pupils need guidance and help in answering the questions or completing the questionnaires in order to avoid the danger of their giving the 'expected' answer.

This approach can be used at subject level or as a part of the tutorial programme in school. It would also provide a valuable link between the 'academic' and the 'pastoral' elements of the pupils' development, which many pupils, and some teachers, still see as separate and quite unconnected entities.

Pupils in Key Stages 1–3

- I find learning most enjoyable when. . . .
- The type of teaching I learn best from is. . . .
- When I do well in lessons I feel. . . .
- The things I have found hard to learn are. . . .
- One particular thing/topic I would like to learn and understand is. . . .
- I can learn by myself if. . . .
- I do best in group work when. . . .
- In all subjects, I feel I am particularly good at doing. . . .
- I sometimes avoid learning because. . . .
- The most recent thing I have learnt is. . . .
- What I should most like to learn about myself is. . . .

(Adapted from Day *et al.* 1988)

Pupils in Key Stages 3–4

Some of the above questions, suitably modified, could be used in addition to the following:

- Which lessons do you enjoy most, and why (subject, topic, type of lesson, etc.)?
- What was your favourite topic, and why?
- Which was the easiest topic, and were any too easy?
- If you had to give a talk on any topic which would you choose and why?
- Which topic did you find most difficult?
- Are there any topics which you feel you need to go over again?

- Which was the most difficult homework topic you have done?
- Were any homework topics too easy?
- My course work would be easier if. . . .
- I feel I need extra help with/time for . . . .
- The aspect of my school work which worries me most at present is. . . .

The Parents' Perceptions

Although it is often difficult to obtain constructive responses from some parents, any responses can be a valuable source of feedback from these important stakeholders. It would be valuable if there were a tradition in the school of seeking parental views. This approach can be used only if parents feel that their views are important and useful and if they understand why their views are being sought.
Questions which might be used include:

- I have/have not noticed any changes in my son's/daughter's work.
- He/she seems happier with his/her work.
- He/she seems to be doing better at. . . .
- He/she seems to be getting less/the same/more homework.
- He/she talks more/less about the work in school.
- The most positive aspects of school work mentioned are. . . .
- The issues about which he/she seems most unhappy/uncertain are. . . .
- Of the work in school and at home, I would like to see more of. . . .
- Other things that I think would help improve my son's/daughter's learning are. . . .

Because of the reluctance of some parents to complete and return this type of questionnaire, their views might be sought through a questionnaire using 'tick-boxes' or 'ringing of answers'. The latter could use questions with a 1 to 7 scale (Excellent to Very Poor). In all cases the language used should be clear and straightforward without being patronising. For those parents whose English is insufficient to cope with the questions, suitably translated versions should be made available.

The Teachers' Perceptions

There tends to be an assumption that we know what teachers feel about the job they do, because they are always willing to talk about it, usually in informal settings. However, a more detailed self-analysis can be a valuable aid in considering the 'team' approach. It is important that members of the team bring different strengths to the team but, ideally, it is equally important that their views and approaches are complementary to the strengths of the other members.

The questions which might be used when attempting a departmental team audit are given below. This approach can be used in smaller departments, even though it may merely confirm views already known or relationships already working well. It is important that all know the reasons for the questionnaire, are prepared for this type of audit and are willing to treat it in a professional way.

Because some of the questions may be misused by uncommitted and/or cynical teachers, it might be useful to do a 'dry run' with a sample of staff to test their views and to obtain suggestions for improvement.

- What I like most about myself as a teacher is. . . .
- I am best in the classroom when. . . .
- The pupils like it when. . . .
- I would describe my teaching style as. . . .
- When I think about the classroom, I. . . .
- I enjoy teaching most when. . . .
- I would prefer to change my teaching style/approach but. . . .
- What I have still to learn about teaching is. . . .
- What I try to avoid most in my teaching is. . . .
- I envy those teachers who. . . .
- I am the sort of teacher who. . . .
- When someone criticises my teaching, I. . . .
- The main things I like to see happen in my lessons are. . . .
- What I most dislike about being a teacher is. . . .
- The pupils seem to learn best in my lessons when. . . .
- I wish I was better able to. . . .
- Most of my colleagues think I am. . . .

In all cases, the questionnaires have to be analysed carefully in order to evaluate the overall view presented. Questionnaires rarely produce a consensus but the responses should give valuable evaluative evidence for the topic being investigated. It is also important to give feedback to those being questioned, not least in order to show that the questionnaire is important to the school, the team or department.

Staffing Issues

APPROACHES TO EMPOWERMENT

A dictionary definition of empowerment is:

> entrusting the authority and responsibility for a task or tasks to another.

The key words in this definition are 'authority' and 'responsibility' and it is these two words which distinguish empowerment from delegation. The decisions that people take for themselves are the ones which they carry out with the greatest enthusiasm. Empowerment is, therefore, a great motivator; it enriches the jobs of others, improves performance and is excellent for team morale. Additionally, effective empowerment relieves the leader of some tasks, which should allow the leader greater time and freedom to be more involved in true leadership functions.

Empowerment is not always easy to implement. It requires courage, judgement and trust in others because the leader still remains ultimately accountable. In these circumstances it is not always easy to give to others the right to be wrong. However, it is worth considering that leaders will be judged not so much on what they do but on what they inspire others to do. The aim ought to be dispensability not indispensability and it should not be feared.

The following are the 'rules' of effective empowerment:

- Look at your tasks; is there anyone else who could complete them better, quicker and/or more easily?
- Decide what can be devolved and to whom;
- Choose someone who can, and ideally wants to, do the job;
- Consider the benefits that empowerment can create for professional development of the empowered person;
- Does he/she have the experience, expertise or training; if not, what support is needed?
- Explain the task – why it has to be done and what is to be done – but leave the method of doing it to the member of the team;
- Jointly set, or ask him/her to set, clear objectives, the performance indicators and the success criteria to be used;
- Ensure that you hand over the authority as well as the responsibility;
- Agree the size of the task, the priorities and the deadlines;
- Ask for completed work not problems, only suggestions for solutions;
- Show confidence in the member of the team; give praise, positive feedback and the credit for the work done.

MANAGING STAFF DEVELOPMENT

The job descriptions for all teachers should include the responsibility for promoting their own professional development; those for middle and senior managers should also include a commitment to helping with that of members of the team. The following issues should be taken into account, not least because of the time and expense involved in professional development activities:

- The training needs, of individuals or the team, need to be identified, particularly for those teachers who are not specialist in the subject/area involved;
- The outcomes of teacher appraisal (performance review) need to be taken into account in assessing training or development needs;
- The proposed in-service activity should be checked carefully to ensure, as far as is possible, that it meets, as closely as possible, identified needs;
- Any staff development undertaken should contribute to:

  - improving the quality of teaching and learning;
  - improving the standards of achievement of the pupils;
  - enabling the team/school to meet its aims;
  - filling gaps in, or improving, the overall professional development of the individuals undertaking the training and therefore of the team;

- Where there is a financial and/or school time commitment involved in the training, the middle manager should discuss with the team member applying:

  - whether the activity meets at least one of the above criteria;
  - the anticipated outcomes of the training;
  - the ways in which the activity will be evaluated;
  - the ways in which the outcomes will be disseminated to the rest of the team, or other teams where appropriate;

- After the training what follow-up there will be in terms of a brief written report and circulation of course materials, if available;
- A means of evaluating the effects of training on the teacher's performance and/or on the achievement of pupils, even if these effects are likely to be long term;
- For middle managers themselves, or colleagues aspiring to such positions, the training needs should encompass all aspects of the role of the middle manager (e.g. activities on the 'management of people');
- A record should be maintained of all in-service activities undertaken by individuals and the team. This is required for OFSTED inspections and the record will also provide a basis for subsequent evaluation of the effectiveness of the in-service training activities; such evaluation may of necessity be long term (e.g. improvement in the pupils' achievement). The record also provides a means of ensuring an equitable distribution of training opportunities.

WORKING WITH TEAMS

A team is defined as a group of two or more people working harmoniously together with common, agreed purposes and goals.

Advantages

Teamwork:

- enables more ambitious and challenging targets to be set, through sharing, devolvement and empowerment;
- allows higher standards and better quality to be achieved;
- helps with security, sanctuary and solace (the three 'Ss');
- gives greater flexibility through sharing of tasks, expertise and time;
- is more than the sum of the parts.

Purposes

Organisations use teams or groups in order to:

- investigate;
- take decisions;
- share the workload;
- monitor and oversee the work;
- solve problems;
- collect and share information and ideas;
- test and ratify decisions;
- co-ordinate and liaise;
- increase involvement and commitment;
- negotiate and resolve conflicts.

Individuals use teams or groups to:

- share in a common activity;
- promote a cause or idea;
- gain status or power;
- gain experience and expertise;
- belong;
- fulfil part of their job description.

The composition, size, organisation, decision-making process and capacity of the team are all affected by the purpose(s) of the work of the team.

Size

The optimum size depends on the purpose or task. It is often a compromise between getting a group small enough to work effectively, where everyone contributes to the work, and big enough to provide sufficient experience, expertise and interaction to generate ideas and cope with the task set. Small groups are more cohesive and encourage full participation; larger groups have greater diversity of talent.

Process

Many of the purposes of the team are fulfilled whilst working together on the process part of the task in hand (e.g. in meetings, discussion and working groups, workshop sessions). The stages in the growth of teams have been defined (Belbin 1981) as:

- 'Forming'   – an often 'edgy' process of familiarisation within the group, during which each individual eventually makes his/her mark, displays a little of his/her agenda and identifies the agenda of the others;
- 'Storming'   – a period of possible conflict, sometimes about the aims of the group, sometimes about the aims of individuals, in which the first easy, but often false, consensus is challenged;
- 'Norming'   – a re-settling into an acceptable way of working with goals and roles more fully understood and accepted;
- 'Performing' – a mature and sensibly productive phase which allows for argument and discussion but within an agreed set of objectives.

Quality Teams

They:

- are driven by a common purpose and set of expectations;
- listen to the opinions, concerns and ideas of others;
- make their values and philosophy explicit;
- regularly review their progress;
- conduct their business with a view to 'fitness for purpose'.

Quality teams need:

- chairing and steering;
- creative inputs;
- the tasks and objectives clearly defined;
- their performance monitored;
- to work with proper constraints and to work well with other teams;
- to achieve targets within deadlines.

The polarised characteristics of effective and ineffective teams are shown in Table 12. Although most teams rarely work at these extremes, leaders should always attempt to guide their teams into the 'effective' areas.

Table 12 The polarised characteristics of effective and ineffective teams

Effective teams	*Ineffective teams*
Informal, relaxed atmosphere	Bored, tense or uneasy
High level of motivation, commitment and confidence without arrogance	Motivation is low associated with task imposition, lack of confidence and commitment
Good personality matches	Personality clashes evident
Shared expertise from a variety of knowledge, skills and experience	Knowledge, skills and experience used for power and domination by individuals
Relevant discussion and high degree of participation	Discussion is dominated by one or two, and is often irrelevant
Tasks and objectives clearly understood and the team are committed to them	No clear common understanding of tasks or intended outcomes
Conflict is dealt with openly and constructively	Conflict ignored or avoided, or it develops into 'warfare' and opting out
Effective communication with active listening by all members	Communication is poor with contributions often ignored or dismissed
Decisions taken by consensus (avoid voting) with an absence of insular attitudes	Decisions by majority (voting), which the minority have to accept, insularity is a feature
Ideas freely and openly expressed	Personal feelings often hidden, criticism is embarrassing
Leadership shared as appropriate	Leadership absent or only from the chair
Discussion is purposeful and objectives are met in a systematic way	Objectives are rarely met, discussion tends to go round in circles without decisions
Targets set are demanding but realistic	Suffer frustration from work 'overload' or 'underload'
Group regularly reviews progress and performance	Group avoids discussion about progress and performance
Expectation of high quality work	Low expectation of the individuals and the group as a whole
Credibility and respect (internal and external) are features	Low level of respect and esteem within and from outside the team
Satisfaction and enjoyment are apparent	Low level of satisfaction and enjoyment

Source: Belbin (1981).

Team Leaders

Effective team leaders have the following characteristics:

- participative style;
- shared responsibility;
- aligned with agreed purpose;
- high level of communication;
- focused on the future;
- relevant talking/contributions;
- active listening;
- creative talent;
- rapid response.

(Adapted from Bucholz and Roth 1987)

Team leaders have four main functions when working with their teams:

- 'Clarifying' – communicating efficiently and effectively;
- 'Advancing' – helping the team to progress through the objectives towards the goal;
- 'Recognising' – appreciating the value of people and their contribution to the work of the team;
- 'Sharing' – exchanging information, knowledge, skills and experience; co-operating with, and caring about, others.

'Clarifying' and 'Advancing' are *goal skills*; getting the job done well and on time. 'Recognising' and 'Sharing' are *people skills*; working well with others.

Team Members

Effective team members have the following characteristics, under the same headings/functions:

- Clarifying:

    - have a clear understanding of the task;
    - understand their roles;
    - do not respond to speculation and rumour;

- Advancing:

    - care about the work of the team;
    - are friendly, co-operative and loyal, reducing conflict;
    - accept unwelcome decisions;

- Recognising:

    - accept the contributions of all members of the team;

- Sharing:

    - readily accept new members;
    - share the workload equitably;
    - willing to share ideas, information, knowledge, experience, skills and expertise.

Composition of Teams

Belbin (1981) argued that a crucial determinant of team success is the balance of roles that is available to the team. Table 13 identifies these roles, the contributions to the team made by those having such roles and the 'acceptable' weaknesses that may be concomitant with the 'strengths'. The key element is establishing and maintaining the balance of roles. In smaller teams members may have to take on several of the roles to maintain the balance.

Table 13 The roles, contributions and acceptable weaknesses of the members of a team

Role	Contributions	Acceptable weaknesses
Plant	Creative, imaginative, unorthodox, problem-solver	Ignores detail, poor communicator
Resource investigator	Extrovert, enthusiast, communicator, networker	Over-optimistic, often loses interest
Co-ordinator	Mature, confident, chairperson, clarifies goals, promotes decision making, delegates well	Possibly manipulative
Shaper	Challenging and dynamic, thrives on pressure, has drive and courage	Intolerant
Monitor/Evaluator	Sober, strategic, discerning, sees all options	Lacks drive and ability to inspire, overly critical
Team worker	Co-operative, mild, perceptive and diplomatic, listens and builds	Indecisive, easily influenced
Implementor	Disciplined, reliable, conservative, efficient, turns ideas into action	Somewhat inflexible, slow to change
Completer	Painstaking and conscientious, searches out errors, delivers on time	Inclined to worry unduly, reluctant to delegate
Specialist	Single-minded, self-starting, dedicated, provides knowledge and skills	Narrow focus, dwells on technicalities

Source: Belbin (1981).

While the crucial ingredient for team effectiveness is the balance of team roles, a number of other points need to be stressed:

- The roles are not hierarchical (for example, it is no better being a 'shaper' than a 'plant');
- Most people can operate in more than one role;
- Roles can change over time;
- Roles can change according to the content and context of the work of the team;
- It is possible to develop skills and qualities associated with particular roles.

The Belbin inventory of team roles can help to improve team performance in a number of ways:

- The team can understand its composition, analyse how it works and identify the possible causes of its problems;
- Recruitment to the team can be managed to ensure that the balance of the team roles is consistent with the task;
- Development needs can be identified and latent talents brought into play;
- Teams set up for specific purposes can be designed to optimise effectiveness as long as the task is clear and the team roles are seen as more significant than other existing roles or status;
- Development planning and career succession can be better managed;
- Individual and team reflection can be improved.

Belbin's model provides a powerful tool for improving the performance of teams by maximising the time and energy that is often wasted in coping with the inappropriate relationships of poorly organised teams. If teams are to be effective in the management of the school, subject, department or year group, then team roles have to be given at least as significant a status as position, qualifications and experience; in some cases, effective teamwork may be the overriding factor.

There a number of ways, and training activities, which will allow team roles to be explored and experienced, and thereby more fully understood. This approach will also allow training in the skill areas characteristic of each of the roles. The type of activity for team building will be determined by the nature of the team, because middle managers, although they are leaders of teams, are also a part of at least one other team (e.g. that of subject co-ordinators in a primary school or of year tutors in a secondary school). In addition, there are other variables which must be taken into account:

- a newly appointed middle manager with an already established team;
- an established team leader with a new team or new members;
- an established leader and an established team.

The exercise in *Supplement S4* is one that might be used with the last of these, where a team attempts to review its present position, perhaps because of a general feeling that things are not going well. In all instances of team-building exercises there is a need for the approach to be completely professional and openly honest; otherwise the existing difficulties in the team may well be exacerbated.

A TEAM BUILDING EXERCISE: REVIEWING

The purpose of this activity is to provide information on the team members' perceptions of the workings of their team, as a prelude to possible further action. This type of activity is most useful for a team that meets and works together regularly but wishes to begin to improve its performance.

- Each member is asked to complete, anonymously, a copy of the questionnaire shown in Table 14.

  On the scale 1–10 in Table 14, ring the number which best represents your view of how your team presently operates. Then, using a different colour, ring the number representing how you would like the team to function.

- The questionnaires are collected by a designated person (a member of the school management team might be appropriate, particularly one who works with or alongside the team) who collates and averages the scores. This person might also be asked to complete the questionnaire to give an outsider's view.
- The information is presented to a meeting at which the implications of the results are discussed. The views of the 'outsider' might also be useful as a sort of moderating influence.
- The team must decide what steps need to be taken to improve the way(s) in which the team works.
- An alternative approach is for the whole team to reach a consensus on the questions and then to compare this team view with that of the 'outsider' who knows the work of the team well.

Table 14 Questionnaire on the working of the team

	Objectivity	
We are never objective	1 2 3 4 5 6 7 8 9 10	We are always objective
	Information	
We never get, and use, information	1 2 3 4 5 6 7 8 9 10	We always get, and use, all necessary information
	Organisation	
The team organisation is never suitable for the tasks we undertake	1 2 3 4 5 6 7 8 9 10	The team organisation is always fully suitable for the tasks we undertake
	Decision making	
Our decision-making methods are never appropriate	1 2 3 4 5 6 7 8 9 10	We always make decisions in the most appropriate way
	Leadership	
We are never led in an appropriate way	1 2 3 4 5 6 7 8 9 10	Our leadership is highly appropriate
	Participation	
Participation is always at its lowest	1 2 3 4 5 6 7 8 9 10	Everyone participates fully
	Professional openness	
Opinions are rarely expressed openly and then usually rejected or ignored	1 2 3 4 5 6 7 8 9 10	Opinions are always expressed openly and accepted
	Use of time	
We always use time badly	1 2 3 4 5 6 7 8 9 10	We make best use of time
	Professional development	
This is never a priority	1 2 3 4 5 6 7 8 9 10	This is always given the highest priority
	Satisfaction/Enjoyment	
Work is never enjoyable or satisfying	1 2 3 4 5 6 7 8 9 10	We always get job satisfaction/enjoyment

MANAGING UNDER-PERFORMING STAFF

In order to tackle the problem of under-performance of any member of the team, the following questions need to be considered before a decision on the most appropriate action is taken:

- Why are you concerned and what are the likely consequences for the team, the department/year group, the subject and/or the school?
- What specific issues have led to this concern (i.e. recent facts or incidents without inferences or assumptions)?
- What strategies are available to you in order to help?
- How would you expect the person to react when you raise the issue?
- How would you handle the various reactions, viz. apathy, hostility, compliance, defensiveness, co-operation?
- Can you anticipate the reaction and explanation?
- Can you separate the personal and social from the professional aspects?
- What specific targets can be set?
- Are you the best and/or the only person to seek the answers?

The leadership skill of any manager is critical in dealing successfully with the under-performance of a member of the team (see also Staff Management, pp. 49–50):

- Attempt to maintain and enhance the self-esteem of the member of the team;
- Don't attack the person but focus on the problem;
- Explain to the person what you or others have observed and the concerns you have;
- Encourage the person to express his/her views and to make suggestions; listen carefully and keep an open mind;
- Allow the person time to think through the problem and, if possible, find his/her own suggestions for a solution;
- Express the specific requirements and ensure that possible solutions are translated into an appropriate action plan;
- Offer help and support by you and/or other members of the team;
- Agree the steps to be taken by both of you;
- Always set a specific date for follow-up;
- Don't assume that the person has committed an offence;
- Be aware of the possible need to seek help or to refer the problem to a higher authority at some stage but don't use this as a threat.

JOB DESCRIPTIONS AND PERSON SPECIFICATIONS

All teachers should have a job description which should be reviewed annually. With the introduction of the proposed performance management described in Part 1, the job description is likely to be extended to include target setting phases.

A condition of employment of all teachers is that 'they shall perform, in accordance with any directions which may reasonably be given to them by the headteacher from time to time, such particular duties as may be reasonably assigned to them' (*Schoolteachers' Pay and Conditions of Employment 1999*, DfEE Circular 12/99). This should at least be referred to in all job descriptions although some schools use the conditions given below as a basis for their job descriptions, as shown in the example from a secondary school (see p. 182).

The current conditions of employment for teachers, other than the head teacher, include the following (NB the masculine pronoun is used in the DfEE Circular):

Professional Duties

- Teaching:

  - planning and preparing courses and lessons;
  - teaching, according to their educational needs, the pupils assigned to them, including setting and marking of work to be carried out by the pupil in school and elsewhere;
  - assessing recording and reporting on the development, progress and attainment of pupils;

- Other activities:

  - promoting the general progress and well-being of individual pupils and of any class or group of pupils assigned to them;
  - providing guidance and advice to pupils on educational and social matters and on their further education and future careers, including information about sources of more expert advice on specific questions; making relevant records and reports;
  - making records and reports on personal and social needs of pupils;
  - communicating and consulting with parents or bodies outside the school;
  - participating in meetings arranged for any of the purposes described above;

- Assessments and reports:

  - providing or contributing to oral and written assessments, reports and references relating to individual pupils and groups of pupils;

- Appraisal:

  - participating in arrangements for the appraisal of performance (performance review of self and, where appropriate, other teachers);

- Review, induction, further training and development:
  - review from time to time methods of teaching and programmes of work;
  - participating in arrangements for further training and professional development as a teacher;

- for those serving an induction period, participating in the arrangements for supervision and induction;

- Educational methods:
  - advising and co-operating with the headteacher and other teachers on the preparation and development of courses of study, teaching materials, teaching programmes, methods of teaching and assessment and pastoral arrangements;

- Discipline, health and safety:
  - maintaining good order and discipline among pupils and safeguarding their health and safety both when they are authorised to be on school premises and when engaged in authorised school activities elsewhere;

- Staff meetings:
  - participating in meetings at the school which relate to the curriculum for the school or the administration or organisation of the school, including pastoral arrangements;

- Cover:
  - supervising and so far as practicable teaching any pupils whose teacher is not available to teach them (except after a teacher is absent or otherwise not available and has been absent for three or more consecutive working days); there are other more detailed exceptions which could be included;

- Public examinations:
  - participating in the arrangements for preparing pupils for public examinations and in assessing pupils for the purpose of such examinations;
  - recording and reporting such assessments;
  - participating in arrangements for pupils' presentation for and supervision during such examinations;

- Management:
  - contributing to the selection for the appointment and professional development of other teachers and non-teaching staff, including induction and assessment of new teachers and teachers serving induction periods;
  - co-ordinating or managing the work of other teachers;
  - taking such part as may be required in the review, development and management of activities relating to the curriculum, organisation and pastoral functions of the school;

- Administration:
  - participating in administrative and organisational tasks related to such duties as are described above, including the management or supervision of persons providing support for teachers in the school and the ordering and allocation of equipment and materials;
  - attending assemblies, registering the attendance of pupils and supervising pupils, whether these duties are to be performed before, during or after school sessions;

- Working time – the main terms for classroom teachers (excluding advanced skills teachers) are as follows:

- a teacher employed full-time must be available for work for 195 days in any school year, of which 190 shall be days on which 'he [*sic*] may be required to teach pupils';
- such a teacher 'shall be available to perform such duties at such times and such places as may be specified by the headteacher . . . for 1,265 hours in any school year ("directed time"), these hours to be allocated reasonably throughout those days in the school year on which he is required to be available for work';
- a teacher is required to work 'such additional hours as may be needed to enable him to discharge effectively his professional duties'; these include, in particular, marking pupils' work, writing reports on pupils and preparing lessons, teaching materials and teaching programmes; the division of a teacher's 1,265 hours of 'directed time' between teaching and other duties is for the headteacher to determine.

Advanced Skills Teachers (ASTs)

The new grade of AST was introduced in September 1998 with the following duties, in addition to classroom teachers' professional duties, which ASTs may be required to perform:

- participating in Initial Teacher Training (ITT);
- participating in the mentoring and induction of newly qualified teachers;
- advising other teachers on classroom organisation and teaching methods;
- producing high quality teaching materials;
- disseminating to other teachers materials relating to best practice and educational research;
- advising on the provision of in-service training;
- participating in the appraisal of other teachers;
- helping teachers who are experiencing difficulties;
- working with teachers from other schools, whether at the school of the AST, at that of the other teacher, in higher education institutions, at facilities of the LEA or elsewhere;
- producing high quality resources and materials, including video recordings of lessons, for dissemination in their own school and other schools.

The working time provisions for classroom teachers (as above) will not apply to ASTs.

Examples of Job Descriptions

The following are two examples of 'live' job descriptions, one for all teachers in a secondary school and one for a middle manager in a primary school, in which different approaches have been taken. They are *not* exemplars but could be used as a starting point in considering the production of new job descriptions or the revision of existing ones.

A Secondary School Example for all Teaching Staff

This example is based on the statutory conditions of employment:

> All teachers shall perform in accordance with any directions which may be reasonably given to them by the headteacher.

The teacher shall be responsible for:

- Teaching:
  - planning and preparing courses and lessons;
  - teaching, according to their educational needs, pupils assigned to him [*sic*];
  - assessing, recording and reporting on the development, progress and attainment of pupils;
  - preparing with others courses of study and teaching materials;

- Other activities:
  - promoting the general progress and well-being of pupils;
  - informing parents on a regular basis of equipment required to ensure lessons can proceed;
  - providing guidance and advice to pupils on educational and social matters;
  - recording and reporting on the social and personal needs of pupils;
  - communicating and consulting with parents;
  - communicating and co-operating with outside agencies;
  - participating in meetings arranged to facilitate the above points;

- Assessment and reporting;
  - providing or contributing to oral and written assessments and reports relating to individual pupils and groups of pupils;

- Discipline, health and safety:
  - maintaining good order and discipline among pupils and safeguarding their health and safety both in school and when they are engaged in authorised activities elsewhere;

- Staff meetings:
  - participating in meetings at the school which relate to curriculum, administration, organisation and pastoral matters;

- Cover:
  - supervising and, so far as practicable, teaching any pupils whose teacher is not available to them after the teacher is absent or otherwise not available and has been so for three or more consecutive working days, and if the LEA are unable to provide a supply teacher at this time and have made every effort in accordance with local and national agreements.

- Examinations:
  - participating in arrangements for preparing pupils for public examinations and assessing, recording and reporting on pupils' work in this connection;
  - participating in exam procedures and arrangements for supervision of such examinations;

- Administration:
  - registering the attendance of pupils, attending assemblies and supervising pupils.

A *Primary School Example for the Curriculum Co-ordinator*

NB The feminine pronoun is used in the school's original version.

The Curriculum Co-ordinators have overall responsibility for the teaching and learning in their subject.

To achieve a high standard in both teaching and learning the Co-ordinator must:

- have knowledge of and enthusiasm for the subject, to inform and encourage colleagues;
- manage resources to allow teachers to deliver interesting and differentiated lessons;
- monitor the planning and delivery of lessons and the achievement of the children;
- make provision for assessment and record keeping;
- ensure progression within the subject and coverage of the National Curriculum.

The Co-ordinator is responsible for the development and up-dating of the policy and long-term scheme of work. She is the source of expertise and a resource for other members of staff. She is responsible for the managing of resources including monitoring the care of equipment and, in negotiation with the Resource Manager and the Headteacher, the ordering of new equipment and books. The Subject Co-ordinator should update staff on new developments and advise the Staff Development Manager and the Headteacher of staff training needs. She should liaise with outside agencies, supervising their role at a management level to ensure safety and quality for pupils and staff. The Co-ordinator is also responsible for the monitoring and evaluating of the subject throughout the school.

Medium-term planning is handed to the Co-ordinator each half term. This is assessed by the Co-ordinator in terms of coverage, progression and continuity. The Co-ordinator will discuss with individual teachers any problems which may arise and any ideas which may lead to more effective teaching. Teachers also give the Co-ordinator a list of lessons covered from the previous half term's planning. Educational visits are evaluated by the staff involved who will report back to the Co-ordinator, as are training courses attended by staff. The above information is used by the Co-ordinator to review policy, long-term planning and training needs.

Appointment Job Descriptions

Before appointing any staff to the team/school, a description of the post to be filled should be prepared. Key elements in the description should then be included in the advertisement. Care should be taken to avoid contravening equal opportunities legislation in framing the advertisement and in the more detailed description.

The description should include the essential features required and should be specific enough to attract appropriate applicants but not so specific as to deter other applicants who may offer other experience and expertise, e.g. age range or year groups to be taught and, where appropriate, subject(s) and level or ability range. In addition to the essential features of the post it is useful to add those desirable features which would supplement the work of the team/school, e.g. additional subject(s), help with music, games or specified extra-curricular activities.

When sending further details of the work of the team or the context of the school to applicants, it is often valuable to ask them to write a letter of application on the specific aspects of the post. This may prevent them from using a photocopied general application, which some applicants are still inclined to send.

Person Specification

In addition to a description of the post, it is valuable to consider including a person specification, i.e. an outline of the type of person who would fit in with the team/school culture. The following are obvious examples of what one would want from a new appointment:

- personal impact and presence;
- adaptability to changing circumstances and new ideas;
- energy, vigour and perseverance;
- self-confidence;
- enthusiasm;
- intellectual ability;
- reliability and integrity;
- commitment;
- ability to lead a team and/or work as part of a team.

These are difficult areas to explore at interview and there is a need to rely on confidential references. However, much valuable information can be gained about the candidates' personalities during the informal parts of the appointment process, particularly during informal situations throughout the interview period, and it is here that other members of the staff/team may be able to contribute to the findings.

Having established the criteria for the post and the personal characteristics required, the interview process should concentrate on these. Often the decision on the appointment of the most suitable candidate has to be a compromise and there may be a need to negotiate the actual job description of the successful applicant with some adjustment of the work of others in the team. This last point is sometimes usefully included as a part of the description of the post in order to widen the field of applicants, perhaps through additional comments such as 'there may be opportunities to. . . .' or 'candidates should include any other areas where they have experience or expertise to contribute to the school/team'.

Middle managers should be involved in the appointment process. They might produce the first drafts of the job description or, possibly with a member of the school management team, draw up or review job descriptions for their teams. Where this is done for any new appointment, it is valuable if the middle manager involves other members of the team, for the sake of their professional development as well as getting them to feel a part of the process. This should generate and sustain team involvement and cohesion.

Other Management Issues

MANAGEMENT OF TIME

All teachers have problems of shortage of time both within the classroom and for those many other tasks which form an essential part of the job. Of all the resources available, time is the only one which has absolute finite limits, it is often the scarcest, the most elusive, the one that gets used up most quickly. Recent research, plus evidence from OFSTED inspections and the TTA, has identified that most middle managers, given the time, would do more of what is expected of them, i.e. to lead and manage. Effective users of time rely to a great extent on the planning processes outlined earlier, but so often time is wasted by an over-concentration on the brief contacts and queries and the more routine day-to-day tasks that are common in all forms of middle and senior management roles. The term 'routine' does not mean 'unnecessary' or 'boring'. Routines are established to ensure the success of the team and the school, they are repetitive and predictable and can therefore be planned. However, the increase in statutory administrative tasks, imposed by recent legislation, by the National Curriculum and its assessment and by the periodic impact of OFSTED inspections, has placed additional demands on the time available for all teachers.

Most managers and teachers have some form of 'do it list' (or 'do it today') in order to plan their time. However, these are invariably far too long and list items and issues in an arbitrary fashion, without any indication of priority, importance or timescale. The failing of such lists is that the more difficult and higher priority tasks tend to be relegated while the less demanding and less important tasks are ticked off, simply to reduce the length of the list. This may have some sort of psychological value but if such lists are to be effective they should always include some form of prioritisation and should cover a range of timescales.

The initial list should be items from the team/departmental calendar. This will contain all priority issues determined by the deadlines set for the team as a whole and within which all other activities must be planned. Beyond this the team must determine the other issues which need to be considered on a termly, monthly and/or weekly basis, before compiling the 'do it today/this week' list.

Time Management: an 'In-tray Exercise'

This training exercise is often used to practise the skill of time management. It involves considering a number of issues on a 'do it today' agenda, listing the issues in priority order for action and specifying a start time and timescale for each issue.
A typical list might include:

- An NQT has asked for help with some aspect of the subject which she has to teach today;
- The headteacher informed you yesterday that one of the support staff in your team has resigned; the head wants to act quickly to fill the vacancy and has asked you to draft a job description;
- A student teacher in the team has left you a note to say that three pupils were rude to her in the last lesson on the previous day;
- The LEA Subject Adviser has phoned to make an appointment sometime during the day to discuss what is described as an important issue;

- The headteacher has arranged for a lunchtime meeting with a sales representative who has some new materials which seem relevant and most appropriate for the work being planned as a cross-curricular programme;
- You have received a letter of complaint from a parent about suspected bullying in your class;
- The SENCO wants to meet with you and some other team leaders to discuss a new pupil who may need a Statement of Special Educational Need;
- You have a set of books which need to be marked for the last lesson;
- You promised the PE Co-ordinator that you would help to supervise a team practice at lunchtime;
- At the morning staff briefing the headteacher has asked all subject managers to provide preliminary expenditure plans for the next financial year;
- The after-school meeting you were due to attend at the Teachers' Centre, to discuss new subject regulations, has been cancelled but all those due to attend have been asked to let the Adviser have their views as soon as possible.

Prioritise from this list, assuming that you have one non-teaching lesson on the day. The first step is to prioritise on the importance of the tasks and, second, to decide which tasks may be deferred, delegated (up or down) and done after school. This should create a more useful, and realistic, second list for your 'do it today' list, with the items that are to be deferred given a timescale for completion.

There are no hard and fast rules for the effective management of time. The list given below contains ideas which many managers use to avoid wasting the valuable resource. It is useful to go through the ideas and tick those which will help you, and help you to help others, to make the most effective use of time:

- Remember the vision for the team and keep it in mind when considering priorities;
- Time management is 99 per cent governed by self-discipline;
- Plan your time, don't let it control you;
- Assess the tasks and allocate priorities and timescales;
- Avoid resorting to the quick and easy but trivial tasks;
- Divide the 'large' or difficult tasks into manageable pieces;
- Always ask the planning questions – Why, What, Who, Who for, When, Where and How?;
- Have a daily prioritised 'do it list' but use this in conjunction with the weekly, termly and yearly list;
- Don't overfill the 'do it list' or your diary; other 'urgent', more important issues may arise;
- Use the list, don't be tempted to get side-tracked or to create a secondary list;
- Identify and concentrate on the high yield tasks, if at all possible;
- Whenever possible and appropriate, devolve (but don't abdicate from) tasks 'up', 'down' and/or 'sideways'; agree review and deadline dates;
- Ensure that any meetings are planned to use time as effectively as possible (see also Meetings, pp. 70–1);
- Plan your use of telephone time for outgoing calls and master your telephone technique; it is pleasant and sometimes necessary to socialise and chit-chat but it can waste a lot of time;
- Ensure that the school office knows of your whereabouts and the priority to be allocated to interruptions;

- If a telephone call interrupts a task, make a note of the point you had reached when the call came; distractions can adversely affect the memory;
- Do the least 'desirable' priority tasks first, as they tend to be less unpleasant than anticipated; there is also a psychological boost after the completion of such tasks;
- Be prepared to say 'No'; don't let your enthusiasm outrun your capability to fit things in;
- Spend time in getting it right the first time; repetitions are time-consuming;
- Should your 'open door' be slightly closed most of the time and shut (locked) on other occasions to help to exclude the time-wasters?
- Do one thing at a time, stick to the task and set yourself personal deadlines wherever possible;
- Always have something to do even if it is constructive relaxation;
- Handle paperwork only once if at all possible;
- Read only what you must; learn to scan read and then allocate priorities;
- Use the new technologies whenever possible and appropriate, e.g. personal organisers, ICT, word-processing, the Internet (many large organisations now use telephone and video conferencing to reduce the need for meetings);
- Keep notes and jottings of tasks completed, as these may help to save time if/when these tasks are required again;
- Find some time for thinking (reflection); we all think far more rapidly than we speak, particularly as we think at a conceptual level; individual 'brainstorming', 'charting' or 'mind mapping' of a topic is, for some, a creative and valuable way to record their thinking.

The following list summarises the main points for effective time-management, which is a skill which can be developed through practice:

- Consider and analyse tasks before starting on them;
- Plan what has to be done, who is going to do it, how it is going to be done, when it has to be done, and consider why it has to be done;
- Carry out the priority tasks or delegate them;
- Review progress periodically;
- Instil time management ideas in all of the team;
- Try to save the time of others, but not by doing everything yourself;
- Use 'do it' lists and reminder signs prominently displayed;
- Use stress-reduction techniques (*Supplement M2*);
- Always be on time yourself;
- Always find some 'thinking' time each day;
- Find time to relax by 'coming off task'.

It will not be possible to apply all of these strategies but using even a few of them will allow middle managers and teams to be more systematic in the management of time and will ensure that time is used more efficiently and effectively.

A useful technique to determine time usage by individuals and/or teams is to carry out a type of organisation and management (O and M) review. The method involves recording, or just estimating, the time spent on activities undertaken over a set period. Activities that might be recorded include:

- class/subject teaching – timetabled and other;
- registration;

- pastoral time and assemblies;
- meetings – team, cross-team, school and 'external' meetings;
- preparation for, and follow-up activities of, meetings;
- telephoning – incoming and outgoing calls;
- interviews with pupils, individually and in groups;
- interviews with parents;
- marking of pupils' work;
- other assessment, recording and reporting – identified together and/or separately;
- extra-curricular activities;
- reflection (thinking time);
- movement around the school;
- breaks – totally off task;
- interruptions, including who is doing the interrupting;
- travelling;
- other miscellaneous activities.

This type of audit will not in itself produce answers but it does create questions that middle managers and their teams should investigate in order to make more effective use of the valuable resource of time.

RECOGNITION AND MANAGEMENT OF STRESS

In recent years there has been an increasing use of the word 'stress' because of the extra demands and pressures put on schools, departments and individual teachers. Much of this has arisen from legislation introduced since the mid-1970s, in particular the National Curriculum and its assessment processes and OFSTED inspections. The situation has been further exacerbated by the changes in attitude of the government and society towards schools and teachers. Schools have become increasingly competitive, requiring staff to respond to these external challenges at a time when there are greater expectations, from all quarters, and less resources available to meet the challenges.

This supplement will not provide comprehensive instruction on the nature or origins of stress or on the medical techniques of relieving stress. The intention is merely to draw attention to the signs of stress and to suggest ways of coping, managing and lessening the effects in oneself and in others. Managers should not try to become doctors, psychologists or psychiatrists; where symptoms appear serious, expert professional advice should be sought.

The term 'stress' is used to describe the external demands on an individual's physical and psychological well-being. In engineering terms, loading causes stress and overloading may lead to breakdown. However, the situations which cause psychological stress are more complex and interactive in nature, but 'overload' will appear if an individual's strength or coping strategies are insufficient. The effect of overload differs from person to person; what is stress to one may not be stressful to another. Unfortunately, there are limits when we all feel that we can no longer cope with our stress and it becomes 'distress', but again individuals have their own ways of dealing with the problem.

Stress may be induced by self, by the environment at work and/or at home, or by an interaction between the self and the environment. There are, however, some common misconceptions about stress:

- Stress is bad, negative and should be removed – it is in fact a necessity and is an essential part of life and we have the in-built nervous and hormonal capacity to deal with it;
- Stress is caused by being too busy or pressurised or over-stimulated – conversely, being bored, unchallenged or under-stimulated can be just as stressful;
- Stress is a sign of instability or mental weakness – controlled levels of stress allow us to operate at an optimal potential;
- Change always brings stress – change is an inevitable part of life and should provide the challenge that brings about optimal performance; however, a rapid pace of change, such as that which has been imposed on schools in recent years, has undoubtedly caused increased stress in some teachers although others have risen to the challenges and have been professionally stimulated by the positive aspects of many of the changes.

Characteristics of Healthy Tension, Acceptable Fatigue and Exhaustion

Healthy tension:

- The individual feels well and has a relaxed manner;
- Physical activity and recreational leisure brings pleasure without guilt;
- Burdens and pressures that reduce happiness and may affect health are rejected;
- An increase in challenge and stimulation improves performance;
- The individual is seen as approachable, flexible and full of energy and stamina.

Acceptable fatigue:

- The individual feels and shows tiredness but does not deny it and takes steps to recover as soon as possible;
- Non-essential energy output is deferred;
- Performance can be improved, but greater effort is required;
- Social pressures and mild stimulants such as tea and coffee play a great part in sustaining performance;
- Sleep patterns remain normal;
- The individual is seen as being healthily tired but not anxious because success in performance and job satisfaction are still evident;
- This type of fatigue is healthy.

Unacceptable fatigue/exhaustion:

- The brain becomes less efficient, few problems can be solved on 'automatic pilot';
- The individual is too easily stimulated, becomes hot and bothered about even trivial issues;
- Performance is impaired by loss of energy and stamina, which goes unrecognised;
- There is loss of accuracy and speed of response;
- Discriminative powers deteriorate, time and resources are not managed efficiently and judgement is impaired;
- Loss of leadership skills compels more reliance on status and seniority and there is less adaptability to change;
- There is a tendency to sit around eating, drinking and talking too much and thus indulging in task avoidance;
- Aggression is common and often destroys the goodwill of colleagues;
- Poor coping habits are adopted, e.g. sleep deprivation, denial of major problems, projection on to other people or objects;
- Failure to cope causes feelings of desperation, as the person is unable to carry on but unable to opt out;
- Team organisation breaks down, the individual stops listening to others, loses insight and becomes impossible to work with.

Recognising Stress in Self and Others

It is sometimes difficult to know if someone is suffering from stress but some of the following may be tell-tale signs:

- greater indulgence in smoking, drinking or eating, or loss of appetite;
- difficulty in making decisions and unable to face up to the reality of situations;
- poor concentration and emotional outbursts;
- loss of self-esteem;
- feeling of isolation;
- restlessness, nausea, headaches, muscle tension, dizzy spells, palpitations, general feeling of fatigue or even exhaustion;
- increased heart rate and sweating;
- feelings of anxiety and anger arise.

The Effects of Stress on Work

The individual may exhibit any of the symptoms listed above which may have the following effects on him/her:

- becomes distant from the purpose of work;
- develops negative or cynical attitudes to colleagues and/or pupils and parents;
- avoids contact and relationships with colleagues;
- relies on rules and procedures with a loss of any creative thinking;
- loss of performance/productivity;
- increase in pupil/parent complaints.

The team/school suffers from:

- low staff morale;
- greater sickness and absence levels;
- questionable absenteeism from both staff and pupils;
- decrease in efficiency and effectiveness;
- lowering of standards of teaching and consequently in pupil learning;
- breakdown of pupil discipline.

Managing Stress

In severe cases, or at the sudden appearance of stress, medical help should be sought or advised. However, the skill of the manager lies in recognising the early symptoms of stress and taking remedial steps to reduce or remove the source of the stress if it is work related and within the remit of the middle manager. The senior managers of the school should be involved where the action required is outside the powers of the middle manager.

Some of the causes of stress in teachers are due to organisational issues relating to their overall workload, their teaching programmes, the timetabling or the groups being taught. Through counselling, it should be possible to explore the anxieties facing teachers. This is particularly true of new and inexperienced teachers and care should be given to the demands placed on these members of the team (*Supplement S5*).
The following are ways in which stress might be managed by the individual, the manager or a member of the team:

- List the ways in which you are affected by pressure;
- Plan each day realistically, don't set too many tasks or give too little time;
- Do everything at a reasonable pace and try to avoid hurrying;
- Do only one thing at a time, complete it before attempting to move on;
- If rushing around – stop – think about what you are doing, rest for a moment or two and then carry on more slowly;
- If becoming angry or frustrated with the task in hand, stop and go on to something less frustrating; go back to the task later, it may be less frustrating the second time;
- Think positively and try to see the humorous side of situations;
- Delegate tasks if possible, otherwise ask for help if things are 'getting you down';
- Avoid 'bottling up' all your worries, find a sympathetic ear – it does help;
- When angry or frustrated, try to get it out of your system; express your anger and frustration quietly and honestly if at all possible;
- Work hard for what you want;
- Make a positive effort to rid yourself of those issues which make you feel stressful and upset;
- Take regular, but not necessarily strenuous, exercise; it helps to use excess energy and aids restful sleep;
- Find ways to relax in your spare time (you can always make time); choose other hobbies or interests which are in complete contrast to your work;
- Make best use of weekends and holidays, try to plan ahead;
- Ensure you get enough sleep and rest; try to wind down before going to bed and avoid tea or coffee as they are stimulants – you may sleep but won't necessarily be relaxed since even dreaming can be tiring;
- Seek help and try suggested methods of exercise and relaxation; practise them daily.

(Adapted from a paper, Health and Safety Services, University of Manchester 1993)

Helping Pupils to Manage Stress

Many of the above points of advice in managing stress are equally applicable to pupils who are showing symptoms of stress. Stress in pupils may occur at any time, particularly in those facing their own crises or 'life events', such as teenage problems. However, symptoms of stress will always tend to occur before and during test and examination periods, especially public examinations. During these times tutorial work on managing stress, as well as individual counselling, will prove invaluable in helping pupils to cope better with the anxieties they are experiencing.

COMMUNICATION

Teachers qualify for, and enter, the profession because they are good communicators, able to instil knowledge, skills, ideas and concepts in their pupils. It might seem unnecessary, therefore, to include this supplement on communication. However, the skills of communication required at all levels of management must be of a high standard, simply because of the number and variety of the potential recipients of such communication. All lists of 'standards', including the National Standards, which are expected of middle and senior managers will contain reference to the skill of communication, e.g. 'communicate effectively, orally and in writing, with the headteacher, other staff, pupils, parents, governors, external agencies and the wider community, including business and industry' (*National Standards for Subject Leaders*, TTA 1998).

The problem is that most teachers have little need to practise (and therefore do not) the art of writing, especially preparing lengthy presentations. Most of a teacher's writing is short, usually for personal use only and often in abbreviated or note form. Increasingly, however, written reports and presentations have become a part of the middle manager's role, not least in making applications for promotion.

This supplement has three mains aims:

• to give some general advice on the preparation for writing lengthy reports or for presentations;
• to offer some basic rules on report writing and presentations by managers;
• to highlight some of the common pitfalls, inaccuracies and abuses of English which are likely to lead to misunderstandings, to obscure the meanings and intentions of the writing or to irritate the reader.

Organising information in a clear, concise and logical way can be a rewarding experience. Whatever the purpose of the piece, there should be a planned approach, establishing a title, how long the report/presentation should be and, most importantly, who the recipients are. There is a tendency always to include too much, particularly in presentations, and so the three guiding principles should be:

• accuracy;
• brevity;
• clarity.

The style used must meet the varying needs of the recipients (readers or audience). There will need to be differences in, for example, a report to the headteacher making a case for extra funding, a description of a course of study in a booklet for parents and an action plan following an OFSTED inspection.

The phases in the preparation process are:

• Establish a title and define the purpose carefully – the purpose may already be defined but it must be kept in mind throughout;
• Investigate the subject thoroughly – some find a 'mind map' (*Supplement P2*) useful in that it will not only show content but also give an indication of the interrelationships of facts and ideas;

- Organise the material into sections – try to find linking points between them;
- Produce a first draft quickly, at one attempt if possible – the use of word-processing and double spacing may help in the subsequent editing;
- Ask someone to check the draft for errors and inaccuracies – you may have used the spell/grammar check functions on a word-processor but these are not infallible;
- Produce the final draft, with a brief summary of the key issues as a conclusion.

The paragraph is the best aid to clarity of thinking and writing, and therefore to understanding. The paragraph can be defined as

> essentially a unit of thought, not of length; it must be homogeneous in subject matter and sequential in treatment.

Put simply, each topic or idea requires a new paragraph. Each paragraph should, ideally, begin with a key sentence which will contain the main idea/point to be conveyed. Many busy readers use the technique of reading only the first sentence in each paragraph. Short sentences are clearer than long or complex ones and therefore convey the meaning more accurately. More than one or two subordinate clauses modifying the main clause are likely to cause confusion or to cloud the meaning.

George Orwell used the phrase, 'Keep it short, keep it simple', and went on to suggest six straightforward rules:

- *Avoid the use of metaphor, simile or figure of speech*, e.g. clichés such as 'different ball game', 'take on board';
- *Never use a long word when a short one will do*, e.g. 'use' instead of 'utilise', 'about' rather than 'approximately';
- *Never use a general word when a more specific term makes the meaning clearer*, e.g. name a particular part or aspect of the school rather than simply say 'facilities';
- *If it is possible to leave out a word then always do so*, e.g. the most commonly used extra word is 'very'; reduce 'classroom [or any other] situation' to 'classroom';
- *Never use the passive where the active can be used*, e.g. replace 'good behaviour was shown by the younger pupils on the trip' with 'the younger pupils behaved well on the trip'; avoid use of the impersonal passive, e.g. 'it is believed that', 'it is to be hoped that';
- *Never use foreign phrases, scientific/technical words or jargon*; where there is doubt use a plain English equivalent or explain the term used, e.g. for *per se* use 'in itself' or 'by itself', for *ad infinitum* use 'endlessly' or 'without limits'; there is a fine line between technical language and jargon and this is often determined by the perceptions of the readers/audience, e.g. technical language used for OFSTED inspectors might well be regarded as jargon in a report to parents.

Orwell added a final admonition, however: 'break any of these rules rather than say anything barbarous'!

Another area which causes confusion and irritation is the use of acronyms. Education abounds with examples. While parents may know the common ones, e.g. GCSE (although some still refer to 'O Level'), less commonly used ones, e.g. NRA, TTA, AQA/NEAB, QCA, NVQ, may annoy or confuse. Acronyms are used for brevity and the general rule is to give the full title, followed by the acronym in parentheses, on the first occasion. In oral presentations it is better to use the full title each time.

Other management issues

The following points relate to some of the common errors which appear in written reports and oral presentations:

- *Subject/verb agreement*: two nouns joined by 'and' form a plural, e.g. 'history and geography have two lessons each', but compare, 'the number of history and geography lessons is four'.
- *Demonstrative pronouns*: 'this' and 'that' are often used loosely and it is not always clear to whom or what they refer, e.g. 'The class has missed a lot of lessons with a result that test scores are low and parents have complained. This has resulted in a reconsideration of the problem in order to resolve it.' To what does 'this' refer, and what is 'it'?
- *Comparatives*: when only two items are being considered use the comparative, e.g. 'elder of the two' (not the 'eldest'); 'alternative' is one of two not of three or four, which may be 'options'.
- *Adverbs*: these are, in most cases, put after the verb, e.g. 'the work was completed successfully'. This avoids the split infinitive which some find irritating: 'To never split an infinitive is perfectly possible!' However, in the use of 'well', there is a distinction between 'the course was well designed' (adverb which is not hyphenated) and 'it was a well-designed course' (adjective and is hyphenated).
- *Apostrophes*: these still cause problems in some reports, e.g. 'boy's school' means a school for one boy. However, some plural nouns do take ' 's', e.g. 'children's', 'people's'. Some writers confuse the use of 'it's', meaning 'it is', and 'its', meaning 'belonging to it'.

Other uses/abuses include:

- Only meetings, golf balls and envelopes are 'addressed'; 'the team/department is addressing the need for more equipment' means it is still thinking about buying;
- Use 'study in depth' not 'in-depth study' and 'continuing' rather than 'on-going';
- 'Both' and 'and' should take a preposition, e.g. 'both to GCSE syllabuses [not syllabi] and to the National Curriculum', not, 'to both GCSE syllabuses and the National Curriculum';
- If you use 'would' in the main clause you should use the subjunctive in the subordinate clause, e.g. 'if the team were to opt for a new topic, it would raise standards';
- 'Circumstances' surround something, therefore use 'in these circumstances' rather than 'under these circumstances';
- 'Compare A with B' for differences, but 'compare A to B' for similarities;
- Use 'different from', not different 'to' or 'than';
- 'Which' informs, 'that' defines, e.g. 'this is the faulty equipment that the class used' and 'the equipment, which the class used, was faulty';
- 'Less' is about quantity (less equipment), 'fewer' is about number (fewer pupils);
- The 'last scheme of work' implies that there will be no more, use 'most recent' or 'last year's';
- When 'due to' is used to mean 'because of' it should be followed by a noun, e.g. 'the cancellation, due to illness, of the trip' and not, 'the trip was cancelled due to illness';
- 'Uninterested' means 'has no interest in'; 'disinterested' means 'impartial' or 'objective';
- 'Comprise' means 'is composed of', therefore 'boys comprise three-fifths of the class' is meaningless.

MANAGEMENT OF CONFLICT

Effective schools rely on fostering and maintaining good relationships and, because schools are in the 'people's industry', this task is much more difficult because of the number of possible conflicting interests and issues. The middle manager has to develop and attempt to ensure the maintenance of good working relationships within the team, with other teams, with senior managers and the governors, with pupils and their parents, with external agencies and the community.

The sections on the management of staff and the management of pupils (see Part 1) have covered some of the possible areas of conflict but there are other areas which require handling with care. Middle managers are likely to have to cope from time to time with people who, because of personality, position, status, experience, anger or emotional upset, feel that they can be dominantly aggressive. Every situation where this occurs will have its own context and there are few specific pointers to success in what has to be a negotiated exchange. However, in considering a management approach there is a need to accept that all people have certain rights:

- to be treated with respect as intelligent people with their own capabilities;
- to express opinions and feelings;
- to hold their own beliefs and values;
- to say 'yes' or 'no';
- to make mistakes;
- to say that they don't understand;
- to ask for what they want and to say what they don't want;
- not to apologise for the actions of others.

Having accepted these rights, the manager must endeavour to resolve the day-to-day disagreements between people. One approach is to use assertive behaviour, which is often confused with aggressive behaviour. Being assertive means:

- examining and acknowledging something you feel;
- establishing short-term objectives;
- determining the action that needs to be taken;
- deciding on the process involved in that action;
- reacting in a rational rather than emotional way;
- acting in a calm and deliberate way;
- avoiding the denial of other people's rights.

Often the most difficult situations arise in relationships with parents, particularly when they feel that their child is being singled out, has been hurt (physically or emotionally) or is not being treated 'fairly'. It is likely that the parent will be arguing at the emotional level – with anger and aggressiveness – and will be asking for immediate action. When pressurised to respond immediately, a manager may find the following assertive techniques useful:

- Remain calm, logical and confident;
- Let the person/people talk; angry people often become calm as they unburden themselves;
- Listen carefully and attentively;

- Try to resist the temptation to jump in too early;
- Clarify by asking questions; be sure that you fully understand what is being asked of you;
- Think about and acknowledge that you understand the problem;
- At some stage you will probably have to say 'I can't do that now', 'I need time to sort it out', 'I need to speak to other people', etc.;
- Give a specific timescale for the decision and explain the way in which you will convey the decision or complete the task.

Having been assertive in the face of aggression, or even in a more ordinary situation, you may still not 'win', e.g. where a school policy decision seems not to meet with the team's approach that you have been putting forward. However, if you 'lose', but feel that you have done all that you can, you cannot accuse yourself, or be accused, of being ineffective. Thus any feelings of self-recrimination, associated with being faced with a decision made by someone else, are avoided.

National Organisations

There are many valuable publications available from the DfEE, OFSTED, QCA, TTA and the teachers' associations. While those particularly relevant to middle managers are referred to in this book, others, too numerous to name, are listed in relevant catalogues. All of the publications, together with information and advice, can be obtained from the publication offices identified below.

- Department for Education and Employment (DfEE)

DfEE
Sanctuary Buildings
Great Smith Street
London
SW1P 3BT

General enquiries: 0207 925 5000
Fax: 0207 925 6979/6980
E-mail: info@dfe.gov.uk
Website: www.dfee.gov.uk

DfEE Publications
PO Box 5050
Annesley
Nottingham
NG15 0DJ

Tel: 0845 602 2260
Fax: 0845 603 3360
Textphone: 0845 6055560
E-mail: dfee@prologistics.co.uk
Website: http://www.dfee.gov.uk

- Office for Standards in Education (OFSTED)

OFSTED
Alexandra House
33 Kingsway
London
WC2B 6SE

General enquiries: 0207 421 6744
Fax: 0207 421 6707
Website: www.ofsted.gov.uk

OFSTED Publications Centre
PO Box 6927
London
E3 3NZ

Tel: 0207 510 0180
Fax: 0207 510 0197
Website:
http://www.ofsted.gov.uk/public/index.htm

- Qualification and Curriuculum Authority (QCA)

QCA
21 Bolton Street
London
W1Y 7PD

General enquiries: 0207 509 5555
Customer Services: 0207 509 5556
Early Years Team: 0207 509 5521
Key Stage 1 Team: 0207 509 5516
Fax: 0207 509 6666
E-mail: info@qca.org.uk
Website: www.qca.org.uk

QCA Publications
PO Box 99
Sudbury
Suffolk
CO10 2SN

Tel: 01787 884444
Fax: 01787 312950
Website: http://www.qca.org.uk

- Teacher Training Agency

TTA
Portland House
Stag Place
London
SW1E 5TT

Tel: 0207 925 3700
Fax: 01245 261668
E-mail: teaching@ttainfo.demon.co.uk
Website: www.teach-tta.gov.uk

TTA Publications (and all enquiries)
Freepost ANG2037
Chelmsford
Essex
CM1 1ZY

Tel: 0845 606 0323 (local call rate)
Fax: 01245 280954
E-mail: publications@ttalit.co.uk

- British Educational Communications and Technology agency

BECTa
Milburn Hill Road
Science Park
Coventry
CV4 7JJ

Tel: 01203 416994
Fax: 01203 411418
E-mail: Becta@becta.org.uk
Website: http://www.becta.org.uk
National Grid for Learning website:
www.ngfl.gov.uk
Virtual Teachers' Centre website:
www.vtc.ngfl.gov.uk

- The Stationery Office (formerly HMSO)

The Stationery Office
Publications Centre
PO Box 276
London
SW8 5DT

General enquiries: 0207 873 0011
Telephone orders: 0207 873 9090
Fax orders: 0207 873 8200
Website: www.hmso.gov.uk.

- Health and Safety Executive

HSE   *Tel*: 0208 594 5522
Educational National Interest Group   *Fax*: 0208 591 5183
Maritime House
1 Linton Road
Barking
Essex
IG11 8HF

For LEA Maintained Schools, the LEA is a source of help, support and advice and all LEAs will have policies, guidelines and support materials on many of the aspects of middle management in schools.

For other schools, the Centre for Educational Management (formerly the Grant Maintained Schools Centre; GMSC) and the Independent Schools Information Service (ISIS) provide similar services:

- Centre for Educational Management

Red Lion House   *Tel*: 01494 474470
9–10 High Street   *Fax*: 01494 474480
High Wycombe   *Website*: http://www.ceduman.co.uk
Bucks
HP11 2AZ

- Independent Schools Information Service

56 Buckingham Gate   *Tel*: 0207 630 8793/4
London   *Fax*: 0207 630 5013
SW1E 6AG   *E-mail*: national@isis.org.uk
                                             Website: http://.isis.org.uk

The assistant teachers' professional associations are also useful sources of support and advice:

- Association of Teachers and Lecturers (ATL)

7 Northumberland Street   *Tel*: 0207 930 6441
London   *Fax*: 0207 930 1359
WC2N 5DA   *E-mail*: info@atl.org.uk
                                             Website: www.atl.org.uk

- Professional Association of Teachers (PAT)

2 St James' Court   *Tel*: 01332 372337
Friar Gate   *Fax*: 01332 290310
Derby   *E-mail*: hg@pat.org.uk
DE1 1BT   *Website*: www.pat.org.uk

- National Association of Schoolmasters/Union of Women Teachers (NAS/UWT)

Hillscourt Education Centre	*Tel*: 0121 453 6150
Rose Hill	*Fax*: 0121 457 6209
Rednal	*E-mail*: nasuwt@nasuwt.org.uk
Birmingham	*Website*: www.teachersunion.org.uk
B45 8RS	

- National Union of Teachers (NUT)

Hamilton House	*Tel*: 0207 388 6191
Mabledon Place	*Fax*: 0207 387 8458
London	*Website*: www.teachers.org.uk
WC1H 9BD	

Through headteachers, and some deputies, advice and support can also be obtained from:

- National Association of Headteachers (NAHT)

1 Heath Square	*Tel*: 01444 472472
Boltro Road	*Fax*: 01444 472473
Haywards Heath	*E-mail*: info@naht.org.uk
West Sussex	*Website*: www.naht.org.uk
RH16 1BL	

- Secondary Heads Association (SHA)

130 Regent Road	*Tel*: 0116 299 1122
Leicester	*Fax*: 0116 299 1123
LE1 7PG	*E-mail*: info@sha.co.uk
	Website: www.sha.org.uk

In addition to the teachers' associations listed above, there are associations for all of the subjects in the curriculum and some of these have regional as well as national offices and officers. Lists of all of these associations can be found in the Education Year Books, copies of which are likely to be available in all schools and public libraries.

EDUCATIONAL PRESS/ONLINE NEWS

Admiral House	*Tel*: 0207 782 3000
66–68 East Smithfield	*Fax*: 0207 782 3200
London	*E-mail*: chat@tesl.demon.co.uk
E1 9XY	*Website*: www.tes.co.uk

- *Managing Schools Today*

Questions Publishing Co. Ltd
27 Frederick Street
Hockley
Birmingham
B1 3HH

Tel: 0121 212 0919
Fax: 0121 212 0959
E-mail: hsharron@questpub.co.uk
Website: http://www.questpub.co.uk

- *Teaching Times Website*: www.teachingtimes.com

- *Times Educational Supplement*

Further Reading

Bell, L, (1992) *Managing Teams in Secondary Schools*, London: Routledge.

Bell, L. and Rhodes, C. (1996) *The Skills in Primary School Management*, London: Routledge.

Crawford, M., Kydd, L. and Riches, C. (eds) (1997) *Leadership and Teams in Educational Management*, Buckingham: Open University Press.

Curriculum, Evaluation and Management Centre, *Value Added Projects*, Dept of Education, University of Newcastle upon Tyne, Newcastle upon Tyne NEI 7RU (*Tel*: 0191 222 6588; *Fax*: 0191 222 5021).

Gold, R. and Szemerenyi, S. (1997) *Running a School: Legal Duties and Responsibilities*, London: Jordan.

Hargreaves, D. and Hopkins, D. (1991) *The Empowered School: the Management and Practice of Development Planning*, London: Cassell.

MacGilchrist, B., Mortimore, P., Savage, J. and Beresford, C. (1995) *Planning Matters: the Impact of Development Planning in Primary Schools*, London: Chapman.

O'Neill, J. and Kitson, N. (eds) (1996) *Effective Curriculum Management: Co-ordinating Learning in the Primary School*, London: Routledge.

Ruddock, J., Chaplain, R. and Wallace, G. (eds) (1995) *School Improvement: What Can Pupils Tell Us?*, London: David Fulton.

References

GOVERNMENT PUBLICATIONS

Crown copyright is reproduced with the permission of the Controller of Her Majesty's Stationery Office.

- Department for Education and Employment

The Education Reform Act 1988: The School Curriculum and Assessment (DES Circular 5/89)
Improving Schools (DfEE/OFSTED 1994)
Better Choices: Putting Principles into Practice (ref. CSBC11 95)
From Targets to Action: Guidance to Support Effective Target-Setting in Schools (1997)
Health and Safety of Pupils on Educational Visits: A Good Practice Guide (HSPV2 98)
Home–School Agreements: Guidance for Schools (ref. PPY4 98)
Homework: Guidelines for Primary and Secondary Schools (ref. HGPS5 98)
Implementation of the National Numeracy Strategy (1998)
Target-setting in Schools (Circular 11/98)
Induction Requirements, Process and Procedures for Newly Qualified Teachers (Circular 5/99)
National Learning Targets: Action Plans (1999)

Published annually:
Reporting Pupils' Achievements
School Teachers' Pay and Conditions of Employment

- Office for Standards in Education

Handbook for the Inspection of Schools (1994)
Subject Management in Secondary Schools: Aspects of Good Practice (1997)
Inspecting Subjects and Aspects: 3–11 and 11–18 (each 1998)
School Evaluation Matters (1998)

Secondary Education 1993–97: A Review of Secondary Schools in England (1998)

- National Council for the Curriculum

Starting Out with the National Curriculum (1992)

- Qualification and Curriculum Authority

Dearing Report: The National Curriculum and its Assessment (SCAA 1994)
Value Added Performance Indicators for Schools (SCAA 1994)
Maintaining Breadth and Balance at Key Stages 1 and 2 (1998)
Preparation for Working Life: Guidance on Managing a Co-ordinated Approach to Work-Related Learning at Key Stage 4 (1998)
School Inspection: A Guide to the Law (1999)

Published annually:
Assessment and Reporting Arrangements Key Stage 1 (jointly with DfEE)
Assessment and Reporting Arrangements Key Stage 2
Assessment and Reporting Arrangements Key Stage 3
Assessment and Reporting Arrangements Key Stage 4 and beyond

Benchmark Information for Key Stages 1 and 2
Benchmark Information for Key Stages 3 and 4

- Teacher Training Agency

Consultation Paper on Standards and a National Professional Qualification for Subject Leaders (1996)
National Standards for Headteachers (1998)
National Standards for Subject Leaders (1998)
National Standards for Special Educational Needs Co-ordinators (1998)
National Standards for Qualified Teacher Status (1998)
The Use of ICT in Subject Teaching: Expected Outcomes for Teachers (England, Wales and Northern Ireland) (1999)

- Welsh Office

Departmental Organisation in Secondary Schools (1994)

OTHER PUBLICATIONS

Belbin, R.M. (1981) *Management Teams: Will They Succeed or Fail?* Oxford: Butterworth Heinemann.
Bennis, W.M. (1969) *The Nature of Organisation Development*, London: Addison-Wesley.
Bowring-Carr, C. and West-Burnham, J. (1994) *Managing Quality in Schools*, Harlow: Longman.
Brown, M., Boyle, B. and Boyle, T. (1999) 'Commonalities between Perception and Practice in Models of School Decision-making in Secondary Schools', *School Leadership and Management* 19(3): 319–31.

Day, C., Johnston, D. and Whitaker, P. (1988) *Managing Primary Schools*, London: Paul Chapman.

Fidler, B. (1996) *Strategic Planning for School Improvement*, London: Pitman.

Homerton College (1999) *Good Practice on Transfer and Transition*, London: DfEE.

Jesson, D. (1994) 'Valuable Addition', *Education*, 24 July.

Kolb, D.A. (1984) *Experiential Learning*, Englewood Cliffs, NJ: Prentice Hall.

Neave, H.R. (1990) *The Deming Dimension*, Knoxville, TN: SPC Press.

Index